THE PATH OF ACTION

THE PATH
OF ACTION

Jack Schwarz

Published in Association with Robert Briggs

A Dutton Paperback

E.P. DUTTON / NEW YORK

Published by E. P. Dutton, a division of NAL Penguin Inc., 2 Park Avenue, New
York, N.Y. 10016.

Library of Congress Cataloging in Publication Data
Schwarz, Jack
    The path of action.
    1. Meditation. 2. Spiritual Life. I. Title. BL627.S44—1977 - 248'.4 -
77-2247
ISBN: 0-525-48231-8

Designed by Ann Gold

10   9   8   7

DEDICATED TO
Lois, Charlene, Tamara,
Robert, Rick, Jack, and Michel.

Contents

Acknowledgements

I wish to thank especially Lois A. Scheller for her patience, loyalty, and the many hours of tedious work performed by her unselfishly and with much love and understanding. To Joan Lynn Schleicher for patiently editing and to Robert Briggs, without whom this book would not have been published. To my editors at E.P. Dutton, especially Bill Whitehead, whose enthusiasm made it so much easier to work. To Dr. Kurt Fantl and his wife, Dr. Margaret Adams Fantl, who from the beginning till the end never failed to support and were the stimulating force for writing this book. And to Dr. Joseph Campbell for his fine foreword and his personal advice and encouragement but above all his friendship.

Foreword

TWO BIRDS OF FAIR PLUMAGE, FRIENDS, CLOSE BOUND,
DWELL TOGETHER IN THE SAME TREE.
ONE OF THEM EATS ITS LUSCIOUS FRUIT,
THE OTHER, NOT EATING, WATCHES.

The lines are from the Indian Rig Veda, and they make a point that is of the essence of the teaching of my admirable friend Jack Schwarz; namely, that in the one tree of our living there dwell two subjects: the subject or ego of our doing, our action, and the subject or ego of our viewing and contemplation. We are not to sacrifice either to the other. They are to be known and cherished as friends, close bound, and as such, mutually dependent. Which is to say (and the point comes out strongly in these pages) that "right action" cannot take place without "right knowing" and that neither can our knowing be called "right" if it does not produce "right action."

Saint Paul's famous complaint in Romans 7:19, "For I do not do the good I want, but the evil I do not want is what I do," is, accordingly, the confession of an essential failure in viewing and right knowing, a failure primarily of the spirit, and not of the flesh. For as we read in the words of the Nazarene, Paul's master: "The eye is the lamp of the body. So, if your eye is sound, your whole body will be full of light, but if your eye is not sound, your whole body will be full of darkness" (Matthew 6:22). What most delights and amazes me in the life, the wisdom, and the teachings of my friend is the way in which his words so often illuminate for me the sayings of the greatest masters. Read, for example, Chapter 6, "The Burning and the Loving," and see whether it does not illuminate the words of Christ just cited. We have all heard — and so frequently! — of the *imitatio Christi.* Of what might such an imitation consist? "I and the Father," he is reported to have said, "are one" (John 10:30). Are we to imitate him in that knowledge? If so, then how?

"There is only one God, and I don't care what you call it," I read in one of the early pages of this little book. "There is one universe, and I don't care what you call it. Become aware that only you are present. Only God is present; so are you. Only God is omnipotent; so are you.... Become aware that only God is vibrating; so are you. You are not just a particle in this ocean we call being; you are the whole ocean. As a living being, you vibrate in body, mind, and spirit. Spirit is the vibrational substance by which we move closest to God and have motion as individuations of God."

In Galations 5:17, we are told: "The desires of the flesh are against the Spirit and the desires of the Spirit are against the flesh." And that will indeed be so when the eyes of the bird in the tree of life that watches are turned away from the one that eats the luscious fruit, and the two are no longer friends, close bound, but have gone apart. "Anyone can attain spirituality on top of a mountain," my friend Jack Schwarz declares, "away from all human contact, but when you have to live with people, it has to be practical." Living with people is the first condition and necessity, however, of a properly human life: at first, as child, in dependency, and then, as adult, in cooperative action with others. The bodhisattva way is what such a path of joyful participation, total knowing and total giving, is called in the Buddhist world. That is the beautiful, noble, loving way taught in this disarmingly direct and unpretentiously profound little book, of which the most remarkable qualities are its startling originality and indubitable authenticity. It is not a commentary on revelations; it is itself the revelation of a lifetime lived in the paradisial garden of that tree wherein the two birds of fair plumage dwell in friendship.

JOSEPH CAMPBELL

New York City
July 14, 1976

Preface

I was quite young when I realized that I could do certain things that other people found extraordinary. Because I was unable to learn about the nature of these things from people around me, I began to search for reports of such abilities in books of philosophy, history, and religion. Very soon, I discovered that what I was able to do could be compared with some of the experiences of holy men described in yogic and Tibetan Buddhist writings. There, I found that these abilities were not considered so special; rather, they were regarded as just one aspect of the pathway of life chosen by these masters. I was astonished to discover that they had learned what they knew by disciplining themselves to a life-style aimed at understanding the basic principles and laws of the infinite.

I asked myself how it is that the Western Hemisphere has not brought forth similar teachers and masters. I realized that I would have to study the Western philosophies in order to find the cause of such a void. I went to all the available churches and lectures. At every opportunity, I stuck my head into books of occultism, mysticism, theology, philosophy, and the like. I took advantage of the fact that I had very little need for sleep and therefore could spend more hours in study and investigation than the average person can. My night hours became the most precious of the day. To be alone with my thoughts and my books was wonderful, but after a while, my body began to show signs of exhaustion. I realized that something was missing, but I did not then know how to take care of that exhaustion. If I could heal myself of self-inflicted wounds within minutes, shouldn't the same method work to overcome tiredness and exhaustion?

Suddenly, I realized that what I should be looking for in my reading were people from Western cultures who exhibited similar *abilities* to mine, not just *ideas* similar to those of Eastern philosophy. But I was unable to find many. Why? The Western world spends tremendous amounts of time *studying* philosophies and all other kinds of knowledge, just as I had been doing for quite a while. Of course, I had been intrigued by these studies, but I had failed to see the most important point in all these teachings. It is one thing to study something, but another thing to practice it, to start *living* it! I learned that these Eastern masters had disciplined themselves by rigorous and righteous living and that to keep up this type of living they all had one thing in common: They *meditated!* In this meditation, they were capable of journeying into their inner selves. They set aside a certain time of the day or night to be charged with pure energy and to restore their beings with that energy.

Of course I did not yet understand how they were able to recharge their physical bodies. However, I began to set a special hour of the night to learn to meditate, as I had read in some of the books of yogic philosophy. It took me quite a while to do the exercises prescribed for successful meditation: concentration, breathing, and then the silence. To sit still silently for a half hour concentrating on one thing was difficult for me, a busy, active person. It seemed unbearable. I found myself shifting in my chair, stirring around, and honestly asking myself how this could give me more energy. The whole thing suddenly seemed rather ridiculous, so I knew that something was wrong with my methods. Maybe if I could find points of difference and comparison with Eastern meditators, I might find the solution for my failure to practice meditation.

After considerable thought, I realized that I was living in a hemisphere that has a completely different speed of living and a different economic, social, and cultural value structure from that of my Eastern teachers. I was subject to, or rather a victim of, my environment, which was consciously and subliminally influencing and indoctrinating me and seemingly impressing me with the urge to move with the tremendous speed at which my society was operating. This society had impressed upon me the thought that I would have to become a material success, that such success is the most important factor in life. The average person spends eight hours daily making a so-called living, thinking about practically nothing except how much money to make and the best method to get the most with the least effort.

Most people have an occupation or profession that they aren't happy with, but they continue with it for the sake of making a living. After hours, they try to relax with some sort of recreation; but actually they are not really "recreating" themselves at all, for they are still mentally involved with all the negativity of a world of greed, competition, material fulfillment, and game playing. When they finally retire for the night, another illusion awaits them. Instead of receiving the rest they need, they are more tired the next morning than they were when they went to bed. They drag themselves toward the new day with disgust, knowing that yesterday is going to repeat itself. Scientists, in their latest research, have found that such persons do not really sleep more than a fraction of the time they think they have been asleep. Subconsciously, they have continued to worry about the rat race.

I knew then that if I wanted to be successful in meditation, I would have to adapt myself to a method suitable to our way of living. Because of the tremendous differences between East and West, I could not just copy the methods of the East. I would have to change them, taking from them only what could be adapted to the Western way of thinking and living. Also I knew that the path on which Western society has put itself could not and should not be the path for me. For in all the time that we spend with the material or physical side of life, we do not spend more than five minutes with that which made it possible for us to *be* in the first place. All the things for which we strive come from one source. Very few of us, for example, stop for a moment of prayer before our evening meals, and even those of us who do rarely think about what we are saying. We simply repeat words that have lost their meaning for us. In order to give thanks to someone or something, should we not first acknowledge the existence of such a being or thing and realize our relationship with it, rather than merely uttering some words into nowhere?

These thoughts made me realize that if my meditations were ever to become successful, I would have to understand and consciously apply the principles governing them. Meditation is only a tool, a vehicle to bring me closer to my proposed goal. At that point, my first question — Who is Jack Schwarz? — became unimportant. New questions arose: Who am I? What is my substance? How am I governed? I experienced an intense craving for answers to these questions, a hunger not comparable to the hunger for food, a feeling or deep emotion totally different from anything I had ever known. It was as though an inner voice kept calling to me, but I could not distinguish or understand the words. (Were they words at all?)

As I pondered these questions, a feeling of refreshment came over me, and I decided that this was the time to meditate. Perhaps this time I would get some answers. Inwardly, I knew that this time it would have to be much more than the usual exercises of breathing, concentration, and relaxation. I was aware that I must first empty myself, bringing into equilibrium the complete pattern of my thoughts and actions of that day so that it would not reappear and become part of my actions (or should I say reactions?) in the future. What we are today is the result of what we experienced yesterday, the sum total of all past embodiments here or on other planes of consciousness. I also realized that my future will be based on experiences of the past in its broadest sense. "As ye sow, so shall you reap." It was apparent that I had lived and experienced several different pathways. Now the time had come to create a state of consciousness in which all these pathways could converge and lead to one aim, to one meaning: God. If I could better understand what it meant that we were created in God's image, I would know more about myself and about God.

In my contemplative state, while these questions were running through my mind like a stream of water, I had to take a look at myself. I did not necessarily have to go back into the past, but I did have to take a look at the now. There was an urge somewhere inside me to find out everything about that being called "me." It was a feeling of vexation of spirit, a divine discontent, wanting to know more or, rather, all there was to know about that being I call myself. Now I knew I had to start realizing the day that had just passed, including the reflection of all days of past aeons before that particular day. Encapsulated within my one body, mind, and soul is the sum total of all events, wisdom, and knowledge gleaned along the way. How does one preserve memories and bring them forth to relive or at least review them?

If we want to capture a moment of a particular day, such as a pleasurable visit with friends, we can make pictures or movies so that later we can look at them and recall that moment of pleasure. Similarly, if I took a mental movie of everything I had experienced, I could project it on a mental screen and review and evaluate it in detail. After a few minutes, using my concentration exercises, I was capable of seeing the screen, so I gave the mental order to start rolling the film. Within minutes, the images of the day passed by on the screen as if I were watching a show. I found that I could even slow down the film or stop it and look at the still picture until all details were clear to me. Because I was capable of doing all this, the transmutation process had to begin.

A little earlier, I spoke of creating an equilibrium. I meant that in this universe, with its bipolar energy, everything has a positive and a negative polarity. The balance between the two polarities makes the equilibrium. Where did we lose this understanding? It was when we started to call everything positive "good" and everything negative "bad." By hanging onto the negatives, the so-called bad actions or sins, we created feelings of guilt, and we got out of balance. In the same way, others might hang onto their positives, the good actions, thereby creating feelings of conceit that make them equally out of balance. Therefore, there can be only one answer here: to remove the hang-ups of so-called good and bad, thus restoring balance between the polarities, creating equilibrium.

On the night that I had discovered the process of transformation by review of past actions, I had also realized that I had to rid myself of all attitudes that restrained me from such growth. Guilt and resentment had to be laid aside by understanding how they are created in the first place. When we judge an action to be negative or regret a bitter thought we have had, how should we relate to it during our review of the day? I have learned that it is far better to let go of our grief about it and instead feel great joy. Why joy? Because we have been able to acknowledge an aspect of ourselves that is less than perfect. In our imperfections, we see the challenges to grow, the motivation to keep expanding.

After I had gone over all my experiences of that day as they had revealed themselves on my mental projection screen, a feeling of relief came over me, and also a certain emptiness. I knew I was ready to be filled through meditation. Now it was time to go through the preliminary exercises and then into the silence. For the first time since I had started to meditate, I was capable of entering into the silence completely, without any disturbance. During the silent period, I felt indeed as if I were being filled with new energy, and a feeling of ecstasy came over me. I went to bed for two hours; after I awakened, I felt that I was not the same person I had been the day before. I felt that I had been reborn, with the responsibility to live anew, to treat the world with a completely new outlook, bringing to my work this new energy acquired in the meditation. I had found my method, my way of meditation. I realized that every night, the Jack Schwarz of that day had to die in meditation and return reborn, a new entity, the next morning to accomplish another stretch on his path to fulfillment.

Do I ascribe to any one philosophy? Yes. It is the philosophy of eternal life to be lived by yourself, the realization that you yourself pave the road by which you reach this state of consciousness. All the philosophies of the world are merely signs to let you know of the many crossroads and side roads. But you create your path and set the pace by which you follow it. I assure you, it's an exhilarating feeling to know that no one will have to goad you. It is your inner self that you will answer to and follow. It is therefore vital to know this inner self so well that you will respond to its every desire. It is my conviction that meditation is the best way for me to get acquainted with this higher self. That does not mean it has to be the best way for everyone else. Everyone must find their own method for reaching within.

Since I had found my method of meditation, I was convinced I would also be able to find the answers to my questions. The question "What am I?" returned to my consciousness. I knew that my next meditation would have to bring the answer. The following day, this question occupied most of my thoughts. Although I was aware of performing my normal daily activities, a strange feeling of living on two planes of consciousness started to come over me. At the same time, something else was happening to me. From time to time, I found myself looking down, seemingly from a great height, and seeing myself perform my duties. Awareness of a completely new state of excitement came over me. It was like being surrounded by soft masses of clouds, seemingly dense but supple and transparent, a substance of great plasticity in which I was moving. Finally, it became clear to me that I was of the same substance, and I became aware of an electric sort of vibration and of brilliant colors swirling around me as if I were a ray of light moving through an invisible prism refracting the substance into different colors. The experience was ineffable. I was unaware of time but eventually returned to my state of physical consciousness. I tried to recall every moment of this experience and to understand its meaning.

When the workday ended and I had gone home, I settled down in my room and thought about the experience. I spoke aloud, recalled it, and asked that it be confirmed and clarified during my meditation. During the silent period, there was a flash of white light and, several minutes later, streaks of colored light vibrant against a dark velvet background. The words "You are light" echoed from somewhere within me. Then it was quiet again. Innumerable forms and shapes shining with an electric glow floated through the velvety darkness, similar to reflections on the surface of a moonlit river. Then suddenly it was over. I opened my eyes and looked around, astonished to see that I was in my room. I still had a woozy feeling, and I remembered that I had been meditating. I felt that I was electrically charged and that anything I touched would give me a shock.

Science has said that light is the reflection of energy that is the substance of the universe vibrating in many frequencies. If I am light, I must then be composed of the same energy as the cosmos.

Now I understood that what science calls energy is spirit, or being in action. I, too, am energy or spirit. I was created in the image of God, out of his essence, spirit, or energy. All these are qualities of God. I just had to become aware of them and through this awareness be able to bring them to the surface and practice them in my daily activities.

THE PATH OF ACTION

one

UNDERSTANDING THAT
YOU ARE THE UNIVERSE

Locked within the inner chambers of our beings are our desires, fears, and anxieties but also our inherent potentials for
courage, growth, and self-knowledge. Why is it important that
we bring these hidden aspects to full consciousness and actualize them? Because, as I have often said, we are hoarding
potentials so great that they are just about unimaginable. We
are unaware of most of them; others remain unused because
we cannot find ways to apply them creatively. Most of us are so
controlled by the directives of group consciousness that we are
unable to operate beyond those directions and so are unable to
express our individuality or fulfill our unique creative potentials. Instead of being a society of individuals, we are a society
of joiners, always seeking group direction. Our sense of identity seems to rely entirely on our memberships. Without all
these structures to hold ourselves together, it sometimes seems
that we would disintegrate into nothing.

But there is a revolution occurring, really a reevolution,
which is demanding that we transcend the group consciousness and realize our individuality. To do this, we must unlearn

1

all that indoctrinated us into the group. Education originally meant "to bring forth." We must escape the state of blind acceptance and susceptibility that our education has created within us. We must learn to hear and follow a most clear-seeing and powerful leader: the knowingness within ourselves. That is the only leader capable of transforming earthly existence into harmonious balance by creating harmony within us. We can achieve this inner balance only by bringing into consciousness those latent facets of our beings, those inherent potentials and fears and desires that are hidden in our inner chambers. Creative meditation is a technique that can stimulate and guide this inner awakening. And personal awakening is the first action we must take if we are to attain enlightenment in the world.

LEARN TO OBSERVE YOURSELF
IN ALL YOUR ASPECTS

As I discuss enlightenment as the goal of meditation, I shall use many words that are so common their meanings have nearly been lost. So let me begin by telling you what they mean to me. All things have three aspects: the physical, the mental, and the spiritual or holistic. Now *spirit* means the unadulterated, the pure, the undiluted. The spiritual principle in the cosmos is First Cause. It is not generated by anything; it generates everything. The soul is the spiritual capacity of the individual by which each of us has our being; it is the vessel that holds our spirit and thereby forms our being. The *mental* principle is the inherent quality within spirit that directs the energy coming from the spiritual vessel or soul; it is the mind. We call this quality *consciousness*. The *physical* principle, the body, expresses this direction of energy.

Of these three aspects, the soul is the most difficult to comprehend. When we speak of our souls, we are actually talking about those particles of the universal substance out of which we exist and have our being. Some people say that they have seen the soul leave the body when someone dies. That tells us that the individualized particle of universal spirit is composed of an intangible kind of matter. Actually, we could call it matter, but because it is invisible to us, we do not usually recognize it to be matter. Nevertheless, the fact that it is intangible should not prevent us from recognizing that it exists. After all, we recognize many other kinds of subtle matter. There are several levels of existence in this universe above the barely physical, and we surely recognize them. There is an etheric layer that goes beyond the atmosphere of the earth, where the vibrations are so high that we can hardly call them matter, but they are real nonetheless. This kind of subtle matter can actually be called music because it vibrates so high in the etheric layer that it resonates as a definite musical sound.

Pythagoras taught about the music of the spheres. He realized that each little, indivisible particle in the universe was vibrating and creating two things through its vibrations: light and sound. Today, we can show that sound is light and light is sound; we have instruments for this. We can even make a beautiful musical symphony and a color symphony at the same time through the use of electronics. Each vibration has its own color, its own reflection of light, and its own sound, and each of its aspects is interchangeable. Vibrations are the soul of light and sound, manifestations of the spirit generating them, which we cannot see or hear. Vibration is, in fact, the universal substance.

Our souls are vibrant. They are made of the universal substance, and they are just as real as any other kind of matter. Our flesh and bones are also made of the universal substance; they are merely denser. In studying the principle of vibration, we know that the higher the vibration, the more subtle the mass; the lower the vibration, the more solid the mass. Our beings are in motion, and as human beings, we are vibrating quite rapidly. We vibrate at a high rate because we have a mind, a governing organization by which we direct the body's vibrations. That governing organization is the thinking process, and it includes not just the conscious thinking process but also subconscious thinking and, to go even farther, the holistic awareness provided by the paraconscious mind.

And what is the *paraconscious mind*? Like the other parts of mind, like the soul and the body, it is a vibration. When it is functioning properly, it operates at the same vibrational level as the mind of the universe, and it is through the paraconscious that we come into contact with the universal mind. It brings us our consciousness of the divine; through it, we experience aspects of the universal mind. We call these experiences intuition, insight, and inspiration. At these awesome moments, we glimpse the meaning and purpose of existence. So the paraconscious mind is very important to us; in fact, all our actions should be directed by it. Sadly enough, I have found that people rarely understand the paraconscious mind. Without such an understanding, we can operate on only the conscious and subconscious levels; very seldom — only by default, as it were — can we operate at a paraconscious level. Most of us function exactly that way. That is why we are in disharmony. We are lopsided; we are using only two-thirds of our minds. Because of our upbringing and education, we have become rigid and don't even believe our own paraconscious mind when it flashes information to us. Even then, unless we subject such data to rationalization and analysis, we do not use the contributions of the paraconscious mind at all.

From the earliest ages, certain people have separated themselves from the accepted group doctrines of their time and become mystics. I divide them into three categories. The first type is the *ascetic*. These people adhere to strict rules of life and are often vegetarian and celibate. They have often reached a level of purity by their simple lives that have made them vibrate like flames. And they have often experienced manifestations of the divine, visions and meditations, that attest to their attunement to the paraconscious mind, to the messages of the universe.

The second type is the *ecstatic*. They reach high levels of vibration through ecstasy. A contemporary example are the whirling dervishes, whose ceremony I witnessed in London.* Dressed in long black and white robes that form a kind of wide skirt, they whirled and whirled for three hours, to the sound of spiritual music. Why do they do this? A scientist could tell us that vibrations in the universe move in a spiral form, creating a vortex. When we create a vortex with our bodies by going around and around, we cause a friction that becomes static electricity. As they whirl faster and faster, these dervishes create an electromagnetic field and thus enclose themselves in a shell of vibrations. Such shells have great value for the paraconscious. For example, I have participated in experiments in which a person is placed inside a Faraday cage† and that person's perceptions of psychic forces and spiritual forces have been increased 75 percent. The static electricity created by the dervishes' movements becomes a kind of human Faraday cage around them. And like our modern experimental subjects, when the dervishes experience a high vibration level, they become tranquil and perceive beautiful insights within themselves.

The third type is the *practical mystic*. A person may not be aware of being a mystic, but through his or her way of living and philosophy of life, that person shows it truly. To be a mystic means to live totally according to a philosophy based on spiritual knowing. Now philosophy may not sound very spiritual, but philosophy is a beautiful spiritual word if we understand and live it. The Greek *philos* means love and *sophia*

*A ritual performed by the Mawlawi order of Sufis, of Turkish origin.

†A Faraday cage is an insulated room surrounded by very fine copper mesh wiring through which a high-voltage current is conducted. This establishes an electric static field around the cage that shields the room from external electric noises such as radio, television, and other electric equipment. It is used in parapsychological experiments and heightens the receptivity of the subject in the cage. See Andrija Puharich's *Beyond Telepathy* (Doubleday Anchor Books, 1973).

means wisdom. So philosophy means love of wisdom. Wisdom is intellectual knowledge transmuted into a complete love experience, a spiritual experience. It is no longer a belief; it is a knowing that is a state of total being. In the Sufistic philosophy, for example, it is said: "My divine insight never fails me, but I fail when I fail to listen to it." This reflects the use of the paraconscious mind, the divine inflow into consciousness from the individuated particles of God, of the universe, within us. So when we say we want to know more about our souls, we are saying that we need to know more about the universe, which we are. Soul is not a small, individual package; it is our total being and partakes of the whole universe. Realize that we are the cosmos, which we can also call God. There is only one God, and I don't care what you call it. There is one universe, and I don't care what you call it. Become aware that only you are present. Only God is present; so are you. Only God is omnipotent; so are you. Only God is omniscient; so are you. Become aware that only God is vibrating; so are you. You are not just a particle in this ocean we call being; you are the whole ocean.

As a living being, you vibrate in body, mind, and spirit. Spirit is the vibrational substance by which we move closest to God and have motion as individuations of God. Meditation lets us perceive the spirit in us, to pass from isolation into the fullness of being.

The techniques and states of meditation differ according to the level of your spiritual understanding, but they all are aimed at enhancing your spiritual growth. Now what is spiritual growth? Being spiritual does not mean entering a monastery or walking along the street speaking the word *God,* holding a prayer card, or saying, "Hallelujah, brother!" When we speak of spiritual growth, we mean the kind of growth that enhances the total being. Without the ability to express and manifest spirituality in our daily living, it has no value; it produces disharmony. Saying prayers at night, saying grace at meals, and going to church on Sunday is not necessarily spirituality, merely religion. To be spiritual, one must work and live as a spiritual being. Spirituality is living according to one's *total* being. You can wash the dishes spiritually if you involve your total being by realizing that you couldn't do anything without this spirit, that you couldn't even crook your finger without spirit because spirit is the energy you live by. On the other hand, the person who is tremendously religious can find evidence for disharmonies in body and mind that show he or she is not acting as a total being and therefore not living spiritually. *Thinking* spiritually is different from *living* spiritually. Just to think spiritually is not sufficient; the body you have been given must express it. Every act of our lives should be an act in which we realize that it is the spirit that moves us in its broadest sense. Whatever levels of growth we have achieved, we must try to act in this way if we are to be spiritual. Meditation, as we shall see, can help us to act in this way. Meditation in this sense is more a matter of *how* than of *what*.

When the total mind—conscious, subconscious, and paraconscious or divine consciousness—is involved in this kind of action, then the body also becomes involved. Arabs have a beautiful tradition to show this. Before they speak, they give a salutation; they touch a hand to forehead, mouth, and heart. This ritual says, "I computed it here [forehead], I speak it with my mouth, but it originates in my heart." Then when they have finished talking, they reverse the motions, starting with the heart, to the mouth, to the head, as if to make sure that what is said by the other person is also coming from the heart, to be spoken by the mouth, and computed by the mind.

You are meant to think before you speak. How many times is your heart involved in what you are doing? Every act should be a spiritual one involving your total being—soul, mind, and body—done for the sake of the doing, given for the sake of the giving, worked for the sake of the working, *not* for the sake of what you can get out of it. The more you do this, uniting all the aspects of your being, the more you will create harmony, balance, and peace. The more spiritual you become, the higher the state of your meditation will be.

To meditate means to apply and use our conscious thought forces in harmonious integration and mutual responsiveness.

Meditation should never become anything other than the means of fulfilling this spiritual purpose. It should never become an escape hatch, a way to rid yourself of the outside world for a little while. Always keep its purposes of harmony and integration in view. In the beginning, we will have to retrain our conscious and subconscious minds to constant harmony. After we have become quite adept in meditation, our bodies, minds, and souls will operate in harmony all the time without the involvement of conscious thought forces. Then we won't have to think, "I have to do this with involvement of my heart," for that is the most natural way of living, to be moved automatically by love and wisdom. But in the beginning we must use our conscious thought forces to orient ourselves to that level of understanding and being.

YOU CAN PURSUE TOTAL BEING THROUGH MEDITATION

Through meditation, we can approach a perpetual harmony of mind and body. Another way of describing that harmony is to call it inner and outer balance. With this balance, we are in harmony with the laws of the cosmos, and the result is total health. Health is not a virtue; it is our natural state. We were created in health, in perfect communion with the law of the cosmos. As we lost contact with our wholeness, our spirituality, we lost the balance that is health. Now, we must learn the law, consciously follow it in order to regain our original state. Then we will no longer follow the law; we will become the law. Our minds, being individualized aspects of the universal mind, will, in the beginning stages of correct meditation, be able to tune in to the higher vibrations of the universal mind and draw all the power necessary for spiritual growth from its energy.

Nature can demonstrate to us this natural order if we take the time to listen. I knew a woman in southern California who had a beautiful rosebush outside her door. She pruned it and took good care of it, but this wasn't the important part. Every morning, before she left for work, she would go to this rosebush, hold one of the roses, kiss it, and say, "I love you." She was temporarily transferred to another office and leased her house to someone else. The person who moved in and cared for the plant didn't know anything about love. He pruned and watered the bush, but it never flowered; the buds would open and wither away the next day. After six months, the woman came back and asked what happened to her bush. He explained that he had followed her instructions. The next morning, she started talking to the rosebush, saying, "I still love you. Please show me some beautiful flowers again so I can kiss you every morning." Sentimental? Why not? Within a week, the rosebush was blooming again because this woman understood the kinship she has with all life.

You should be so close to nature that you sense that it, too, is made of the spirit substance that is actually a part of yourself. You have kinship with all life, but you probably seldom show it to your fellowmen, much less to flowers, trees, or animals. All this life is governed by the same mind, the universal mind of which you are a part. Therefore, you are the plant; we are the trees; our minds have some domain within all these things.

Real spiritual growth is acquiring the knowledge of truth. We might all agree with that. But what is truth? Is it something we can never reach? Or is it right at our fingertips, but we fail to see it? Truth is not a magical formula, nor is it mysterious or mystical. It is what we *are*, what we experience. Therefore, if we constantly search for truth outside of ourselves, we are being foolish. We will never in this life comprehend the total truth because if we could, we wouldn't need to be in this physical body anymore. We would have found perfection. Truth is that which the universe is, the absolute truth, the infinite. We are still finite. Only when we can come to the complete realization of the totality of the unmanifested universe will we know total truth. But now, at this moment, we can know what is truth for ourselves by recognizing every experience in our lives, regardless of its level, to be truth. It is a changing truth, changing every fraction of every second of our lives because we are experiencing life in fractions. We cannot even measure the time by which we experience truth. Whenever we add to our experiences, our truth is expanding, and we can say that we are growing because the growing process itself is part of truth. So the knowledge of truth means nothing else but becoming aware of our own growth.

Creative substance or spirit manifests itself through mind and matter. This prime substance creates a tool from itself to express itself in another mode. Mind acts as an instrument or medium of prime substance, like a receiving and transmitting station. I am speaking here of the totality of the mind, not just a portion of it. The essential characteristics of prime substance are energy and motion, which produce a variety of forms of life and activity. This in itself indicates that the creative substance is alive. Something that is not alive cannot produce something that is alive. Actually, the creative substance could be called life. It isn't just alive; it *is* all life. There is nothing in this universe that could ever be called lifeless. It is all progressive motion.

The concept of the Trinity, found in many of the world's religions, can help us comprehend this universal life. You are using the Trinity in every thought and every action of your life, for you cannot live without it. God, or the Father, is the cause, the creator; the Son is the effect. A cause will never create an effect unless something happens to that cause. In order to make the effect, an action, a motion, an energy, or a vibration occurs that activates this cause. We cannot have an effect unless we have a cause, and we cannot have an effect from a cause unless will or desire moves us. That desire, in the Christian scheme, is the Holy Spirit. That spirit is your action, your motion, your vibration, and that which makes you move. Everything that is, is in motion and acts in accordance with the symbolism of the Trinity.

It is so wrong to talk about death as stopping everything. Existence never stops because the finite is created out of the infinite. Prime substance expresses itself infinitely through mind and matter. It never stops expressing itself — *never*! Spirit may at times seem to us to have stopped expressing itself, but that is just because we are so limited in our own senses. Our notion of a solid is relative to our vision. We now have the technological means to show steel to be a liquid mass and to realize that when you put your finger on a table, you may think that you are just putting it on a table, but you are really merging with that table.

So, creative or prime substance is life. Within itself, this creative substance contains a law through which the production of its diverse expressions takes place. This is the law of cause and effect, action and reaction. By examination of the inherent law of creative substance, we find that it is essentially progressive. All that we have learned, whether we practice it or not, is part of our experience; it is knowledge that cannot be taken away from us. When we add wisdom and knowledge to experience, we will grow. We will find that everything in this universe is progressive, even though it may not appear to be.

We could also speak of the progression of cycles. The only reason we are becoming more aware of it in our own era is because we actually are approaching a new age. It is of utmost importance that we understand why we are in such a revolution. It looks like a mess now because we are in a preparatory stage. Astronomically, the earth's polar axis completes a cycle every 25,868 years. This is visible by the position of the sun at the time of the vernal equinox as it is seen against the background of the zodiac. Each zodiacal sign measures 30 degrees of the sun's apparent path through the sky and the vernal point precesses along this path, moving into a different zodiacal segment every 2,160 years. These time periods seem to be connected with major social epochs in the history of humanity. For example, since about 100 B.C., the vernal point has been in the constellation of Pisces, a water sign. The new religion of this age, Christianity, has the symbol of the fish.

Now the vernal point is approaching the constellation of Aquarius, the water-bearer, which is an air sign. The circulatory system is ruled by this sign. Because the heart is where the spiritual and physical powers come together, the circulatory system symbolizes the dissemination of the benefits of this union. In the Aquarian Age, we will have a complete, harmonious expression of what we truly are. That is why we speak of the spiritual revolution. We are preparing ourselves to manifest the heart of being, as we enter the spiritual age.

THE LAW OF LOVE

We think of love in a very limited way. The law of love is manifested differently on each level of existence. For example, at the atomic level, love is expressed by magnetic attraction between opposites. All things manifested by the creative substance have negative and positive aspects. Among animals and human beings, we refer to this duality as gender, and love is expressed as desire between the two sexes. The union of the two results in the procreation of similar forms of matter. Because animals and humans are individualized parts of the universal mind, they have an individualized desire for reproduction and an individualized desire to fuse, to join again in the wholeness from which they came.

When I speak of fusing and merging and attraction and desire, let us realize that sex is just the expressive part of it. The expressive part is always the physical part. If we talk about sex, we should emphasize that attraction and desire should arise from the spirit substance. That is, the souls should be attracted to each other, rather than the bodies. The souls want to merge, and this desire forms a mental rapport between these two manifesting individualized entities. Sex without the attraction of the soul, without the mental rapport, is even below the animal level. There has to be a complete fusing, a merging of the total substance, manifestation, and finally the expression. Therefore, any sex act that is not operating within the law of love is not complete. We see it in our society today. We think we can express love through physical sex only, without the involvement of soul, without the involvement of mental rapport. We tend to equate love with mere physical satisfaction.

We should, of course, realize that the expression of love is not limited to reproduction; reproduction simply is one reflection of the principle of love. Attraction and desire can and should be expressed in many ways, in the union of minds through rapport, in the merging of souls meeting in spiritual communion.

We must enlarge our limited vision of the world in order to experience the cosmos. Unless we expand the peripheries of our beings beyond our own narrow little worlds, we shall never know what the cosmos is all about. Usually, we just ignore it; and in that, we are truly conceited. A good cure for this false pride is to visit a planetarium or observatory and look at the magnification of our own galaxy. How difficult it is to find the sun, which supplies us with all the energy to live by; how impossible it is to find our own planet. If you remember that there are billions of these galaxies, you will realize how small we actually are and how big the cosmos is, that cosmos about which we talk so glibly and unconcernedly.

The cosmos is functioning very well; all its parts are operating together. But because it is unapparent to us, we don't know anything about it. Still, we want to be involved with it. So we take a first layer of that cosmic jigsaw puzzle, and we bring it down. We call this process *analysis*. We actually grab the puzzle from the shelf, throw the pieces on the floor, and then start looking at the pieces. Now all the pieces are separated, and therefore we are lost. But we want to know how it was, so what do we do? We pray a little. That means we go down on our knees and start picking up the pieces. Praying is going into action; prayers should change the situation. By that action of going on our knees to pick up the pieces, we become the mediators between the organized and the disorganized. We call it *meditation*. Meditation is a cry for help to that unapparent state, as if to say, "Hey, place out there, will you become a little bit more apparent so I can live you, experience you, be you? Make me your instrument." This works. Take my word for it for the moment. It works.

So, you reach the point where the pieces are together again. Now there is only one more action to follow: synthesizing. You have put the pieces back, but now you must put a frame around the puzzle so that it doesn't fall apart. This distance, between you and the world (outside you and inside you), which was at first unapparent to you, has become apparent because of your efforts. That is how you know more about the cosmos. You have experienced it, taken it out of its unapparent state, made it disorganized (which is not necessarily negative), gone into action, and put it back together.

You ask: "How can I do this? How can such a thing possibly work?" The efficacy of meditation depends on the paraconscious mind, the universal mind that is immanent and alive in the universe and in you. All that exists comes from the paraconscious universal mind; it is the root from which everything derives. You float in this universe like a cell floating in lymph. Your nucleus is your individualized paraconscious mind. As the cell receives its nutrition from the surrounding lymph, so you get your nourishment from the universal fluid in which we have our beings. This fluid is what we call spirit. So spirit is the prime substance from which all other substances are derived. This is why your body is contained within your spirit, not the reverse. But your spirit has thoroughly penetrated every cell of your physical being. Scientists have partially realized this in their discovery of the two chemicals RNA and DNA, which are nutrifying chemicals and which communicate energy between the brain and the cells. Each cell thus contains all of your life; it has the memory pattern of your total being. And just as DNA and RNA are immanent and complete in every cell of your body, so the universal paraconscious mind is immanent and complete in every being, including you. You may have forgotten it; you may have insulted it by neglect; but it is still there, permeating your being. Spirit is immanent in everything — in your kidneys and your big toes, and the craters on the moon.

Let me illustrate. On many occasions, someone has said to

me, "You're out of your mind, Jack," placing a finger on the forehead, as if this is where the mind is. But my mind is everywhere in my body. It permeates it. What about that mind that is in my little toe? That is why it is strange for someone to say something like, "My kidney is ailing." What does the person mean by that? If your kidney is sick, then you are sick in totality because you cannot consider one part of your body outside of the context of the whole body. If your kidney is sick, then your little toe is sick, too. Everything you are is sick.

When we say that something is "sick," we mean that an aspect is not at ease. We say that it is "diseased" due to the disharmony of the body and of the mind. This happens because we have lost our awareness of the universal paraconscious mind individualized within each of us. The mind is just a tool of the spirit substance, meant not to express but to manifest. Expression, whether of illness or anything else, should happen only after awareness enters in, and then it is on the physical level. Remember, I make a firm distinction, one to be kept in mind at all times, regarding the tripartite being of man: Spirit is the essential substance, mind is the manifester, and the body is the expresser. Spirit permeates mind and body. Meditation opens the spirit, the universal mind to us.

You can recognize only one thing to be the real authority, to be supreme, to be what you call God. The prefix *para* stands for beyond, and so the paraconscious mind is the authoritative knowingness that is beyond the subconscious and conscious mind. It is our constant, continuous, perpetual connection with the total universe, with God.

It is precisely because of our lack of awareness of the paraconscious mind that we do not perform as total beings, that we go about lopsided, in disharmony. People often speak of mind and body as if they were two separate entities. Body and mind can never be separated on this planet. I am talking about this physical episode of our existence from which we may grow to other episodes that might not be physical at all. We can return or be recreated in a different form or shape. Recall for a moment what you've seen of water transformed into snow. Could we ever see water separated from snow? Without the substance of water, there would be no snow in the first place. Snow is only a form into which water can be transformed. Mind (here I mean the totality of mind, not of any particular part or division), then, is like water that is transformed into snow. The universal mind, which is impersonal, becomes individualized within each human being; it becomes a personal mind. Through the action of the universal mentality, spirit is transformed into matter and by the same means into its personal identity or body. This is why I believe that our individualized minds created our bodies; our minds and souls were already existing before the world existed. We are actually cocreators of this physical world. It should not be so difficult, then, to understand that the mind is not a material, physical organ within our individual bodies. Mind is contained in every cell of our bodies. Or we could say that our bodies are actually mental because our minds are the manifesters of spirit substance.

This, of course, is the hermetic philosophy. The entire universe is mental, meaning that the spirit substance can only express itself by means of intelligence and mentality. There has to be a governing agent that activates the universal substance, the spirit, to manifest itself. That governing agent is mind.

As a manifestation of mind, you are an endless being, a cosmic being, an eternal being. What you know consciously and unconsciously is microscopic compared with what you can grasp through your eternal paraconscious knowing. Many people imagine that when the body dies, the mind automatically dies. Let us for a moment go back to the snow. What happens to the water when the snow dies? What happened to the essence? The water still exists, doesn't it? When the snow melts (dies), it returns to its original substance or takes on another form. It can become steam, but it is not the snow that becomes steam, it is the water. The same is true with the body and mind. The primary substance never ceases to exist; it transforms and manifests itself according to the level of existence, whether it be the physical or the spiritual level. Death, therefore, is merely our term for the metamorphosis of eternal prime substance, mind. Once we realize this, it should be clear to us that the mind should master the body, rather than that the body should master the mind.

Have you ever realized that what is contained in our subconscious minds has been gathered through all our existences in different forms? Because we are now in human bodies, the subconscious mind will throw out the information pertaining to this physical plane. Just for the sake of an analogy, let us say that I have in my subconscious mind a thousand pounds of information from all lifetimes that I have lived on the physical plane (regardless of whether it was on a lower level of existence, in the plant world or in the animal world). All that information is with me. Where did I get all the information? I obtained it from the physical plane, from this planet, which in itself is just a microorganism in the total universe. And all this information is just a fraction of a fraction of this microscopically small planet, the earth. If I can just draw information from the totality of the universe, from the paraconscious, even only an amount as small as a mustard seed, it would be several billion times heavier and more powerful than my thousand pounds of information and than all the information available in the subconscious mind of the total earth. It is by meditation that we can begin to draw that little grain of energy from the universe, which we must do in order to move our mountains and live up to our full potentials.

All experiences go into what I call the *pool of wisdom*, the universal archives from which we can draw whatever we want. But you are your own library card; your mind is your entrance key. It vibrates on a certain frequency, that frequency on which you are now existing. Your particular frequency opens the gate to that particular section where you will find the books or records appropriate to that level on which you are existing. You can always read the books on the lower development levels, but you will never be allowed to tune in on the higher levels unless you have the capacity to bring in those higher vibrations. If you wish to read more books in the universal library, you should start evolving so that you can tune in to those more highly developed books.

We have spoken of metamorphosis, of the end of one form and the beginning of another, both having the same substance. When we speak of the beginning, we can refer only to the beginning of each individualized manifestation because the prime creative substance (spirit, God, cosmos, universe) has neither a beginning nor an end. At our level of existence, we can see the universe as existing from eternity to eternity. Therefore, because we are the universe, we, too, are living from eternity to eternity. There is never an ending to your being. There might be an ending to your physical being, but your soul, your prime substance (the God within), lives from eternity to eternity.

When spirit individualizes, an entity is formed by involution. This is very important. Like any seed, this entity always has all the potential capacity, abilities, aspects, and qualities of the totality of the blossom and the fruit. The forward progress of this entity to higher levels of existence is called evolution — in another word, growth.

The planting of the seed obviously comes before growth. Ask any farmer about that. It is very clear, then, that involution always precedes evolution. There has to be an inflow before there can be an outflow. A bottle must be filled before it can be emptied. Involution, the encoding, the planting of the seed, precedes evolution, the process of growth.

Thus, we must assume that the protoplasmic entity, your personal spirit, is actually a potential idea, or seed. Potentially, it has all the evolutionary processes already within it, but it must be stimulated in order to express them. This innate ability to express is the potential mentality of the individualized prime substance. The vibratory level of the potential creative idea gives quality to the individualized spirit.

This brings us then to the mental characteristic of the prime substance, that is, to the involvement of the creative universal mind in the process of creation. The prime substance forms the spiritual essence of a person. This spiritual essence, or soul, through its union with matter, produces a form, or body, that is the expression of the soul. This is why I say that we find the body within the soul rather than the soul within the body. This body still floats in the prime substance in all its forms, in all its shapes, and in all its being. Actually, your body even floats within all the material substances surrounding you. You are in direct contact with all that exists, in spite of what the geographer or the astronomer calls space or time.

Therefore, for example, when you say that you travel astrally, you mean that you were actually always there but that you have just become conscious of it. You are at this moment everywhere throughout the universe, but you are not conscious of it. You are as much in Tibet as you are in your home, and you are as much at the North Pole as you are at the South Pole. You have just not become conscious of it. All that you are experiencing, even reading this, has already happened when you become conscious of it. As a matter of fact, you are not even here anymore; you are at the moment awakening to something that is going to happen consciously to you in a short time. You are already experiencing this, for there is no such thing as time in the universe. There is only consciousness, and we have to become aware of this consciousness to experience truly.

Let me be clearer about this business of space and time. The future is not a future. It is already there, and it is already happening. This is why some people can foresee the future. They have become conscious of what is happening now, which through our concepts of time looks like the future. In most cases where the prophecy fails, the perceiver is unable to interpret the multidimensional occurrence into three-dimensional language. The entire universe already is; we just have to become aware of it. Seemingly that takes time, but time per se does not exist. We are traveling through this consciousness that is our evolution. We can travel through this consciousness as fast as we desire, faster than the speed of light. Experiencing is consciousness. I am sure that some people would argue this point with me. Again, I say that this is what Jack Schwarz thinks it is. Don't be convinced, for then you will have taken it on my authority. I don't want you to take anyone's authority. The only real authority is your own inner truth, the truth that stems from the paraconscious immanent within you.

How can we distinguish the voice of truth from that of misleading opinion? We must first realize that there is a very big difference between creative discovery within yourself and logical verification. The logical way of verification is to rely upon the discoveries of someone else and to acknowledge that other to be the authority for determining what is true and what is not true. A good example of creative discovery is making practical use of your dreams by looking upon them as the reality that they mask. That would give our whole being a chance to pursue its most powerful urges and to change. Dreams are important. The imagery that occurs within your dreams has specific meanings for you, and if you could act them out in your daily life, you might derive a totally different meaning of life than that which you reached through logical verification. We have found that we can solve problems in our dreaming. If we approached our dreams creatively, then we would realize that at the same time a problem is created, its solution is created. We might be able to solve these problems in full consciousness. But because we are dominated in our perceptions by the restrictions of rationalism, we pursue the problem and allow ourselves to become identified with it. Even though we say that we are looking for a solution, in reality we are hanging onto the problem. The solution lies within the unconscious. You *know* the solution already.

A good example of the creative discovery process is the story of the man who found the schematic formula for proteins. He had gotten half of it through his normal thinking process.

Then he dreamt the rest, and upon waking, he knew he had seen the whole thing. So he said to himself, When I go to sleep again, I will dream it. But this time, I will wake up immediately and write it down; I will put the diagram on a piece of paper. And so he went to sleep, and in the middle of the night, he woke up and got the picture of the whole thing, wrote it down and went to sleep again. The next morning, he remembered that he had been dreaming, but he didn't remember writing the dream down. He was very surprised to find the whole formula written on a piece of paper, and if he hadn't recognized his own handwriting, he might have thought that some entity had flown in and done it for him.

Think how many times you could do the same thing! Just put in your mind the thought that you want to wake up at a specific time and rely upon your biological time clock. If you really need to, you will wake up at that time. Sometimes you can make your dreams work for you by giving your mind an order about the problem you want to solve. You have been focusing upon that problem for so long that you can't see the solution. But in sleep, you release your conscious grasp on the problem, and its solution can float to the surface. You knew it, you see, all along.

Let me summarize the distinction between logical verification and creative discovery. Logical verification manipulates the concepts we have learned in the past according to the rules of rational thinking. That process gives us no more than we started with. In creative discovery, we use more than these concepts. Concepts are blended with paraconscious perceptions to take us beyond the limited awareness that created the problem or perpetuated our ignorance in the first place. We perceive by resonating with the universal paraconscious. This resonance forms a tension with the contents of our unconscious mind, our past experiences. When that tension is tapped and when the percept integrates with former concepts, a new idea is formed. That new concept has been derived from the process of creative discovery and is more than the sum of the parts.

Only by intuitional experience can you waken to the paraconscious and transcend the bottleneck of logical consciousness. What do you think? What do you feel? What do you know? What is the difference between these three questions? The first one is based on logical verification. The second is based on feedback from the senses and the body; emotions are involved, too. The third one is derived from experience, but it is not a complete description. It is really intuitional experience. It is difficult to verbalize those things that come intuitively; that is creative discovery. You know, and you know that you know, but you don't know *how* you know that you know.

Let me give you an example, one that I have used for many years. I was driving from Portland to Seattle, and I saw the road sign that says Seattle. So I knew I was on the right freeway. Suddenly, I knew that I had to get off that freeway. Now don't ask me why because I couldn't tell you. I just knew that I had to get off. The person sitting next to me said, "Hey, why are you getting off the freeway?" "I don't know," I said. "Well, why are you doing it then?" "Because I know I have to." Now, if I hadn't had my car radio turned on, I might never have known why I did what I did. A couple of minutes later, it advised people traveling from Portland to Seattle to take a particular exit because the next five miles were blocked by a traffic accident. If you ask me for a logical explanation, I have none to give you. But if you wish to know why this happened, I would say that I had been in tune with intuition.

As I have said, I see an individual's awareness as having three aspects: One is the conscious mind, one is the subconscious mind, and the third is the paraconscious universal mind. Now, how does the mind perceive? Through the five senses. Is that the only way we perceive? Let me give you another example. My nose smells coffee. I once had an experience of coffee that tasted bitter and burned my mouth. I might never want to taste coffee again. Now that my sensors tell me the same or similar situation is present, the drawers of my mental filing cabinet start to jump open, and immediately the past information is displayed. This conceptual response will tend to determine whether I allow myself to have the experience. Now if I have the capacity to allow the intuitive to enter, I might transcend the logical response that the coffee might burn my mouth again and remove the fear that may direct my actions. Then I may learn more about the coffee: that it can burn but that it can also be very pleasant to taste.

At all times, we are drawing in percepts from the cosmos that enter our paraconscious minds. There these percepts are nourished until a certain need pushes them to the surface, into the conscious mind — *if* we give them the opportunity. We may have allowed our intuitional filter to clog. It's like living in a house with three rooms: the kitchen, the living room, and the bedroom. Now, if you pile so much furniture in your living room that you can't see the door to the bedroom anymore, for the rest of your life you might sleep on your couch. And all the time, there's a fantastic, beautiful, spacious bedroom right behind the furniture. You have just forgotten that it is there.

two

GROWING TOWARD
ILLUMINATION

I said in Chapter 1 that I believe we can perceive things in a more real sense if we can use all three of our paraconscious capacities: intuition, insight, and inspiration. Intuition means being in tune with any part of the levels of existence. Insight means becoming aware of what we are in tune with. What is the next step? Bringing the insight into action. In order to allow yourself to start expressing the insight of the intuitive in a practical way, in a life expression, you need fire or inspiration. Inspiration lies beyond logical thinking.

For these three to come to the surface, we have to go through the unlearning process. Our education has blocked what is at the intuitive level in the paraconscious mind. So we must develop the capacity to bring intuition to the surface, *first,* to get insight and, *second,* to start expressing it. Only then will the light begin to shine.

Let me apply the law of Pascal here, the law of communicating vessels. Let us suppose that we have three differently shaped vessels and that they are all connected to each other — communicating, we can call it. Now, if I allow fluid to come into

24

one of these vessels, what happens to the others? They react. Does their reaction depend on form, shape, or anything? No. The liquid will reach the same level in all the vessels unless I block off one of them. If I do that, the fluid will run back and reach a higher level in the other two vessels. This is what we do to the mind by closing off one of its parts. Intuition cannot act if it does not have access to the conscious mind, which has been blocked off from the subconscious mind. Question yourself. Do you rely more on logical verification or on your intuitive nature?

MAINTAIN YOUR BALANCE

We have to establish a proper balance and rhythm in all three aspects of our being. So long as we keep giving more value to one (logical verification) than to another, we lose the equilibrium that is so essential for our whole system. We ordinarily establish rhythms that are not very rewarding to us. Let me give you examples of a rhythm that hinders and one that helps.

First, there is the *erratic rhythm.* It happens whenever we give more value to one viewpoint than to another. When we do that, we are holding onto the pendulum, making it lose the power it needs to swing all the way back. There are people who base all their actions on the negative, giving everything a negative interpretation. There are also people who say, "I only look for the good in people." That means they are blind to things that are not of same nature. Even though these people look for the good, they always wish to improve upon the good they find because they sit in judgment. They are busy minding other people's business, spirits, minds, and bodies. Instead, they should be looking after themselves and their own balance.

Then there is the other rhythm, which I call the *mobile rhythm.* It is a perpetual rhythm, always in motion. Unlike a pendulum, this movement needs no inertia to collect energy. Such a power is so strong that wherever it starts from, it moves straight through and keeps going. A person with this rhythm has gone beyond the law. He no longer has to spend time deciding whether something is right or wrong, positive or negative. This person's aim is clear and directed by paraconscious insight. There is no need for duality to show the way or of concepts to tell that it is right. This effortless effort is the expression of the true harmony of body, mind, and spirit that we must seek.

We can develop erratic rhythms even when we have the best of intentions, even, for example, when we try to grow. We should never become fanatic in our attempts to grow. We should never become so involved with any single step that we forget the purpose of the whole journey, which is very easy to do, particularly when we begin to use certain training techniques to develop some aspect of ourselves. Any technique can be as detrimental to us as it can be helpful if we let it dominate us. That is why it is important for us to remember to use the techniques but never allow them to use us!

When you find yourself caring more about how perfectly you execute the exercise than about the experience it generates within you, then you are dominated by it. Have the courage to change to new methods or adapt the old ones when they become dominant. Any technique, any teacher must be left behind if they are successful in their function and you are true to your purpose. Let them at all times be instruments for you, tools that help you to attain illumination.

What does the word *illumination* mean? When you become more creative with your soul substance, you will start vibrating higher. As you vibrate higher, the color circle of all the vibrations will speed up and suddenly become white light. That is illumination. Then, as a highly vibrating human being, you will always have this light surrounding you, and you will see it and feel it.

Many people say there are bad influences in their environment. Yes, there are. In fact, the only way to protect ourselves against such bad influences is by light, by becoming aware and vibrating so high that we expand and emanate this light (which we are) into our surroundings. If we push aside all darkness, there will be light. Then no negative force can enter because the light that we emanate is a light that operates on a vibration so high that positive and negative have merged and work in harmony.

For example, when I counsel for an entire day,* I must check on my light. If I didn't, I would attract all the problems of the people who come to me, and I would experience all their physical ailments. The first thing I do every morning is sit on the edge of my bed and create a shield of light around myself. In the beginning, this is an act of conscious imagination, and I realize this.

We think that imagination is something bad. We seem to be ashamed of our imaginations, and we suppose that an intellectual person should not act according to imagination. We think that we should know everything out of books, that we don't have to know things by feeling as long as we can explain them. Show me one physical thing in this world that man has created entirely with his hands. Show me one item that was not first conceived by imagination, by intuition, or by thinking power. Therefore, I use my imagination in the beginning to see this light. Yet once I see it and can spread it around me, I become practically surrounded by a force field of high vibration, and no darkness can enter there.

When I become exhausted, I know that I had better check on my light. I close my eyes for a second; if I see that I do not have the light there, I sit for another five minutes and again create it around me. I even place it around my family, for I know they are not always as disciplined as they should be. I visualize them for a few minutes — again, in my own imagination — and put the light around them.

True illumination means that we work with what we are, that

*Jack gives courses in Voluntary Control of Internal States in colleges and universities throughout the United States, as well as private consultations to individuals with problems of a physiological, emotional, mental, or spiritual nature.—*Editor.*

we work to increase the vibrations of the light, which we are. There is nothing mystical or mysterious about it. We derive our values, concepts, and inspirations through introspection and contemplation. Then we manifest these in experiences in the objective, material world. But in order to become creative and productive in the material world, we first have to be subjective and find the time to dwell within the depths of our inner beings to become aware of the real values of life.

What are these values? I think that each individual must answer this. The real values of life certainly are not what society thinks they are. The value that society seems to dictate is to gather as many material things as possible. Many people spend at least ten to twelve hours of the twenty-four hours of the day either acquiring possessions or taking care of them. Yet we know they probably won't last as long as we do. At the same time, we do not spend two minutes a day on things that are of enduring value.

Oh, yes, some of us are very good members of religious congregations. We say a blessing at the table, but we can hardly wait till the blessing is finished; for already our forks are going to our mouths. But to say thank you? Why should we? After all, isn't everything for us? Yes, everything is for us. *But what are we doing with it?* No person on this planet is going to do anything without first knowing what the reward will be. How sad to insist that rewards be tangible things, things that can be seen and touched and maybe put in the bank.

Society also tends to dictate that we become certain kinds of persons, and we worry about this so much that we wind up not becoming anything. This sort of predicament reminds me of the story of two apple seeds placed in the soil at the same time. One apple seed thinks, I have to become a strong tree. I have to grow. So right away, it begins absorbing the nutrition from the soil. Its only thoughts are to become a strong tree and to make the most of what it has. And so the first apple seed begins to grow. But the second apple seed thinks, I wonder, after I have become a tree, if my apples will be red or yellow? I wonder if they will be dry or juicy? I wonder if they will be sweet or tart? I wonder if there will be at least one hundred pounds of apples on my tree? I wonder if my second harvest will be twice as much? Well, the first apple seed is already a tree and is being harvested for the tenth time while that second apple seed is still trying to create a root because it wasted all its energy thinking about what it would get after it had grown. It never spent a thought upon the growing itself.

Society has also made us commercial. We won't do anything unless we get paid for it in society's commercial terms. Before we go to work in the morning, we want to know what we can get out of it. We want to know how much we are going to get paid for it. Or we say, "I am not going to do anything for that person; he's never done anything for me." If the 200 million people in the United States would just spend fifteen minutes tomorrow morning—say, from 9:00 to 9:15 — sending loving thoughts to everyone in this world, armies would put down their weapons at 9:15 and would pray, "Thank you that it is all over. Now I know what love is!" Instead, we hate others; we send out thoughts of hate to our enemies because they are killing our soldiers. But they are not killing them, *we* are killing our soldiers. We are killing them by our thoughts, by hate, by resentment, and also by always wanting to have more, by living only for the tangibles rather than for the spiritual values of life. Only with these values as a foundation, can we build our objectives in the outer world.

Meditation leads us to the inner workplace. Meditation is a creative act that can lead us to the place where the pilot light of the flame of life burns at all times, the flame at the heart of the pyramid. The philosophies of the East speak of the sacred fire, the serpent fire, the kundalini at the center at the base of your spine. Those who have meditated may have experienced this light. Often, the first thing that happens in meditation, after the eyes close, is a vision of a dark shaft that looks like the barrel of a rifle. At the end of the shaft is a pinpoint of white light. Anyone who has ever looked through the barrel of a rifle knows that it is bored in a spiral, a vortex, so that the bullet spins as it exits.

I have my own notion that our nervous system is similarly constructed. We know that the spine in the human body is like an inner spiral of the circle of the cerebral system, that the nerves branch out from the spine, and that at the base of the head is the pituitary gland. This is what I call the spiritual eye. What are we actually seeing in meditation when we see that dark shaft with its spiral and a little spot of light in the end of the shaft? In my opinion, we are looking at the flame, or kundalini, at the base of our spine.

The pituitary gland is looking down the spine as if it were a periscope. When we look inward, during concentration, we visualize the kundalini, the pilot light, which is nothing else than the concentration of the light energy of the universe, and we visualize the spiral, which is the vortex of energy going around the spine.

Now if during meditation you become high (to use a modern term), then you raise these vibrations, and that pilot light becomes a flame. Where there is concentration of energy, vibrations quicken, and the heat is created. When the flame rises higher and higher, it expands and becomes light. Just think about a candle flame; it is hottest, not at the top, but at the base, where the wick is ignited, because that is where the energy is concentrated. That is why people sometimes become very uneasy or itchy and then experience a feeling of heat at that part of the body where they sit. It is very uncomfortable to sit on a hot spot. This indicates that they are actually concentrating tremendous energy there but have never learned to diffuse or emit it. They have an inflow of energy but no outflow, and yet they are surprised when they get headaches from such a compression of choked energies.

The spiritual light comes in through the pineal body, goes

down to the sacrum, and then comes up in a vortex and should be expelled through the forehead. When people can do this, I say that they're wearing their mine worker's helmet with the big spotlight on the front. That is the highest vibration possible on the human level. Therefore, when I speak of the pilot light, I mean this entire cycle of inflow, concentration, and emission of light, the potential of all life.

I've been asked, "Are there lower qualities and forms of this light, too?" Yes, there are, and they produce what we call *psychic sensitivity*. We perceive psychic phenomena through the medulla oblongata, which is the lobe anterior to the occipital bone. The light enters the medulla oblongata, goes down the spine, then comes up along the sacrum, and is expelled from the solar plexus. These are the lower vibrations, the intuitive powers by which we perceive what in our physical world appear to be psychic phenomena. If these lower vibrations are not expelled from the solar plexus, they concentrate in the stomach, causing churning and bloating. If this energy continues to increase, it rises toward the head and puts tremendous pressure on the neck, where it stops.

How many times have you heard someone say, "People are a pain in the neck"? Well, they certainly are because they are sending vibrations at you all the time, and you do not know what to do with them. If you don't expel them from your solar plexus, they become a pain in the neck. We cannot stop people from sending such vibrations, either. Our protection from any negative or difficult situation is in our own sense of balance. Only we can create that balance within ourselves and become invulnerable.

Now you understand what I mean by the pilot light. It will be up to you to turn it up higher until it becomes the bright, radiant, clean, pure light of truth. It will shine in all corners of your being, leaving no room for shadows of doubt. It will, indeed, bring enlightenment. This enlightenment should be not a once-in-a-lifetime experience. Every moment of the day should be enlightened if you make this concentrated energy decentrated so that it flows back into the universe in a creative manner, thereby adding strength to ourselves, to the world, and to the universe. This is indeed a concept of grandeur. You take the light of creation, the universal light, in yourself, and you amplify it and pour it back into the universe by your own creative action, reciprocating through expressing your own growth, your own truth of being.

Illumination can only be expressed in our total beings: spiritually, mentally, and physically. As the body needs nourishment to sustain the physical aspect of being, so the mind needs spiritual and mental nourishment in order to keep spiritual growth intact. Realization of the self then matures by the transmutation of knowledge into wisdom. This is a critically important transmutation. Knowledge is intellectual knowing, and wisdom is spiritual experiencing of that intellectual knowing. As long as you know something only intellectually, you are in a state of believing things that can be changed at any moment; you take intellectual knowing on another's authority, relying on the process of logical verification. In spiritual experience, you take only your own authority, and that is wisdom.

If I were to take you to a river and tell you that the river is water and the water is wet, you might believe me, for you have heard that before. You have been to other rivers; you have been in the rain; you know that water is wet. So you might walk away from the river and take my authority that this particular water is wet, too. But you will never know whether I spoke the truth unless you go to the river and go into the water and get wet. Then your intellectual knowledge is not just a reasonable belief; it has been transformed into an experienced reality.

This is true of the motivation for meditation. It is not enough for you to take my word for its efficacy. You need to know the goal you are working for; you need to *experience* it. Now if you try, and you are open, you will see, you will be inspired. You will receive revelations in meditation that are of a pure inspirational nature, and your conscious mind will have nothing (or at least *should* have nothing) to do with it. Pure inspiration comes as a power of thought, and in order to become aware of these inspirational thoughts, it is essential that you become a clear channel through which your inner cosmic power can flow freely. If you are going to meditate (and I say this seriously), prepare to open yourself for revelation.

What is a revelation? We talk about it, and we hear about it. We read in books about mysticism that some mystic or saint had a revelation. We have revelations every day, but we are not aware of them. And their beauty will never be known to us unless we work for it.

Viktor Frankl has written of his experiences in the Nazi prison camps and of the many people he saw die there. I was in those camps, too, and the only reason each of us came out is that we had one thing in common, a goal. We couldn't die yet; we were not ready to go; we had a purpose to fulfill. We made meaning out of life. Many people are making meaning out of life for the first time. They do it by revelations, by insights into their true natures. They feel so much better because they are living their capacities. They are living to deserve that revelation, for they have seen what one could become, just as I saw in prison camp what I could become. I am grateful that I went through it because I couldn't be here today, being what I am, if I hadn't had that experience. Through suffering, through revelation, we learn to be. That is the meaning of life. Our primary value in life should be to become godlike, to know ourselves and realize within our being and life all the truth that comes to us through inspiration.

If we are manifestations of all-knowing spirit, then there is nothing impossible on the human level. All the aspects of human nature can be brought out, and we should deny ourselves none of these. We do not realize that by denying aspects of our nature, we deny God the experience of life through us.

The ancient Christian traditions speak of God creating us to please himself. God without the universe, God without expression, is nothing. The universe was created to manifest God. Through our minds, intelligences, and intuitions, we can reciprocate and express this creativity.

Perhaps you can recall from your own experiences when growing up that you never learned to express your true self because you never listened to yourself. You never realized (and probably never had a chance to realize) that to express yourself, you have to be *self*-disciplined — that is, literally, self-taught. And you must be self-trained, too. Both come through meditation because you must learn concentration, proper breathing, and relaxation before you can begin to hear your paraconscious mind.

The results of meditation go far beyond self-expression in the vulgar, conventional sense. In every good meditation, you die. When you come out of meditation, you are spiritually reborn. Every meditation should be a dying process. You should never come out of the experience exactly the same person you were before. Some progress or perception should be made physically, mentally, or spiritually. You should be vibrating on a plane that is at least slightly higher than the plane you were on when you entered the meditation.

If you were to ask me why I meditate, I would say that I want to die. I want to die! I want to die out of that state I am now in, to discover that other part of me, to evolve. Let it never happen that the Jack Schwarz who approaches you tomorrow will be the same Jack Schwarz who approached you today because that will mean that I have become stagnant. I should be able to observe the growth that takes place. You need never fear that you will not grow in consciousness. You always grow in consciousness. The only things that might not seem to grow are your awareness of growth and the practical expression of it.

Death becomes much easier to look at when you go through a daily experience of it. The original mode of baptism still practiced in some faiths was not to sprinkle water over a person's head but to dunk the person under the water in order to simulate the experience of death. The neophytes had to go into the void, to know what life and death were. Then they would be able to understand why they had to survive, why they had to act. I pray for the day when humanity realizes this. For we will have a better understanding of our fellow human beings when we have finally begun to vibrate high on the plane of our divine selves, our paraconscious minds.

Some of us are farther along than others. I can go into a room and feel the pains, burdens, pleasures, and loves of the people in that room. I have insight into them, and I can adjust myself to them. I can help someone in need. But there are also those who are not in need of *anything.* I can find peace with them, for they are vibrating on a very high level. You might have felt this high vibration coming from people. Such people fill every corner of the room with their prescience. There are giants like that in our midst, people who are really capable of emanating such vibrations. They are the ones you go to and suddenly feel a peace come over you. You feel relaxed, and yet you are very excited. Such people may never perform any paranormal feats, but their simple beingness expresses their high level of existence and beauty. They have an important role to fulfill. They are the fulcrums of our society; from them we can get extra strength. I call them the reserve batteries of the universe. If you come into their environment when there is something wrong with your own battery, you throw your invisible jump wires to their battery. You pull a little bit of their vibration into yourself so that you can start running again. And it is your challenge to try to become one of these people.

So if we understand the awareness of communication with universal life, we can also understand the sense of immortality. With a greater involvement of our paraconscious minds, we can find this sense. We are absorbing knowledge of those who lived hundreds of years ago. Whatever they were, whatever they acheived by thought or by action, is still in this universe. This is what *immortal* means.

WHAT ARE YOU LOOKING FOR IN MEDITATION?

Perhaps your goal is to still your conscious mind. But if you still your whole mind, you will become entirely stagnant. What you really mean is that you want to stop the interference of the conscious mind with other parts of the mind.

But if you do only this and no more, you will get nowhere except to charge yourself up. I have known many people who expended tremendous effort to meditate and, instead of receiving any benefit from it, became more irritable, more disgusted with themselves. I've told them that they shouldn't meditate because they use meditation as a method for getting more energy. These are the sorts of people who become very restless during meditation. They can't still their bodies, and their thought patterns keep interfering. I have told some of these people not to meditate anymore because they have an excess of energy. Some of them may say, "I didn't meditate last night because I was too tired." Did you ever ask yourself whether you were too tired because you lacked energy or because you were carrying around an excess of energy without putting it to work. It's like having a battery that stands in the garage. Every night, you connect it to a battery charger. After charging it up, you unhook the battery charger and leave the battery where it is, never connecting it with an engine so that it can start generating. You can be tired from carrying surplus energy around within you because you don't allow it to flow. And in most cases, people are more tired from an excess of energy than from a deficiency of energy. But they are not capable of putting that excess energy into some creative expression. It's like saying, "I'm in such good shape that I feel lousy."

In talking about these people, I have been discussing only

one particular kind of meditation, really a preparation for meditation. In this preparatory meditation, we sit and sit and sit, trying to get our minds blank, at peace, quiet, and thereby charged. We should use this type of meditation to reenergize and revitalize ourselves. After you have revitalized, you move to the next stage of meditation, which I call *creative meditation,* in which you start to discover creativity within yourself by unlocking the intuitive. Use both your conscious mind and your unconscious mind. Don't cut off the conscious mind; give it a job to do; make it part of the practice, a part of the aspect of creativity.

As you create, you pass to a new stage. How will you be able to deal with that? Meditation itself will be your greatest ally if you can make it so creative that you start realizing what the changes are that are always taking place within you.

Do not expect your process of enlightenment to be painless. One of the first insights we must have is about the true nature of suffering. It is not a negative experience. All philosophies have taught that enlightenment comes only through suffering. But this does not mean that you should create suffering to speed the process. As soon as you do that, you will resonate on the same level as all the suffering in the world and thereby attract it to you and become attached to it. That attachment will make it impossible for you to transmute the suffering into insights, the proper function of such pain.

Through suffering, we can achieve a higher state, an awareness of the meaning of a greater order of events than those that seemed to cause our distress. When we achieve such understanding, we release the emotions that have been clogging our energy flow, making us have a dense, low vibration. When we learn to annihilate the causes and ways of pain and clogging, we partake of the flux and texture of the cosmos. Then we become cocreators, transforming that which is dense into pure substance, spirit. We become radiant beings. Often in meditation, we feel that we are floating. It is true. As we become more in tune with the universe, we expand our energies into the spaces around us, and the pull of gravity on our bodies is actually lessened. Eventually, this energy can vibrate so high that you will be able to displace the molecular structure of all things that are dense. This is the essence of white magic and one of the unfulfilled potentials of human energy.

three

REDIRECTING YOURSELF
TOWARD MEDITATION

There are three essential preparations for meditation: concentration, relaxation, and regulated breathing. If you practice these elements and make them a part of your daily living, you will bring yourself a way of life in which you project your inner self to the outer world and reflect the outer world within yourself. Thus, these are not just exercises used to prepare for meditation or to reach inner peace and quietude. They can be much more.

Before we concentrate, relax, and regulate our breathing, it is wise to run our hands over the outside world, as it were. The first thing to do is to make your memory project all the things that have occurred during the day. Everything should pass by on a mental projection screen; let it roll along like a movie, and observe very objectively what is being projected, what *you* are projecting on the screen. In this way, you will be able to judge and evaluate the positive as well as the negative sides of your actions on that particular day. Whatever you observe to be entirely negative, you must look at again. Stop the movie, make the picture still, and then look at it. Make an effort to see the positive side of that same action; for the object of this whole undertaking is to transmute the negative into the positive and, indeed, your whole potentiality for the negative into a potentiality for the positive.

REGISTER
YOUR NEGATIVE ACTS

Let us be clear about the fixity of actions. Nothing we do in our lives can be washed away. If what we have done is negative, it can be transmuted into a positive thing. Similarly, a positive thing can be turned into a negativity. But whatever it is, it is always in the universe, it has an existence. For exactly that reason, it can teach us and help us toward a higher level of awareness. It is so very important in this life that we bring all our actions into a harmony, that we create a whole out of all the things we have done. That is why we wash out our minds every day before we go into meditation: to see what we have to deal with.

This first step is one of the most important parts of your meditation. The transmuting of all your negative acts of the day into positive acts creates you anew and moves you beyond what you were by expanding your own understanding. If you are going to build, you must not build guilt, fear, anxiety, or resentment in yourself. Your reward for transmuting these feelings will be that tomorrow you will be acting positively on the negative acts of yesterday. The first positive profit from any negative act or aspect is not a feeling of guilt or repentance but an awareness of it and its negativity. Don't try to create more guilt within yourself; that only enhances negativity. What I am saying is that *true* repentance is more a matter of common sense than of sackcloth and ashes. You need first of all to be aware of your shortcomings; through that awareness, and with earnest effort, you can then outgrow them. Repentance does not mean to feel guilty, to weep over your failures in a flow of self-pity. It means that you know that through awareness you will overcome them and learn self-forgiveness.

We forgive ourselves because we have the godlike power within us to forgive ourselves for our negative acts. Note that I have not used the words *wrong* and *right* or *bad* and *good,* but *negative* and *positive.* These terms do not, and should not, have any moral connotations. They refer to the two poles of a continuum within the universe. Whatever has a negative aspect has to have a positive side, and whatever is positive has to have a negative side. Harmony in the universe demands these two truths.

GIVE UP YOUR GUILT

Thus, we should never leave a feeling of guilt within ourselves; we should learn instead to forgive ourselves for what we know we have done negatively. Guilt itself can only restrain growth. We can grow only through the interchange of positive and negative; therefore, they are equally valuable to us *if* we use them correctly. Our positive actions and experiences are already the fruits of what we did negatively before. Perhaps we cannot learn directly from our virtues, but we can expand our actions in the positive range by going through our negative aspects and becoming aware of them, acknowledging them. For example, we may have been doing the same thing negatively for ten years, but when we sit down and watch our projection screen, we suddenly become aware of this negativity. This recognition is in itself a positive act. So we have begun the transmutation of negative into positive, a transmutation that is completed when we begin to act in accordance with that new perception. In this fashion, the lessons we receive from our negative acts become aspects of our beings, positive aspects. Our futures are based on our experiences in the past; hence a more positive future can only derive from a more positive view of the past.

Consequently, you must not hold onto the negative experiences of the past. Concentrate instead on growing. Be grateful for all the results of your actions. The important thing is that you achieve both an inner and an outer control and an inner and outer harmony. As soon as you reach the stage where you are able to evaluate your actions and are benefiting from both aspects of the past, you will move toward growth and attainment of the higher levels of consciousness and therefore toward the higher harmony. Merely wringing your hands will not accomplish this. How many times have you heard someone say, "Oh, I am so sorry! I feel so ashamed for what I did." Actually, you know this person is asking for your sympathy. The person wants to be punished and is asking you for a slap in the face. This person is not capable of saying, "Well, okay, I made a mistake. I'm not perfect yet. If I were perfect, I wouldn't need this physical body anymore." Life is a lesson. You do not need to whine about your mistakes; you should expend your energies correcting them. You should learn to take your mistakes, your negative acts, with as much grace as you do your positive acts. After all, you could never perceive a positive act unless you knew what the opposite is like. The main thing is to become consciously aware of your negative acts and then restore yourself by becoming positive in your actions.

In Holland, we have a saying that a donkey only stumbles on the same stone once. I do not know what we humans are, then, for we seem to stumble on the same stone a thousand times. We must all be worse than jackasses. As it happens, though, there is an aphorism that is useful for us here. Mabel Colins, in *The Light of the Paths* (Theosophical Press), says, "Before the eyes can look at the master, they have to become incapable of tears." This means that before we can look in the eyes of the master, we must wash out negative self-concerns to that last drop whose passing makes us completely pure. And *you* are the master. Are you aware that you are looking in the eyes of the master every morning when you comb your hair, powder your nose, or shave? How dare you look into the eyes of the master if you are still capable of tears? There is another aphorism in that work: "Before you can speak to the master, the mouth has to become incapable of wounding." Is your tongue in such control and your mind in such control that you do not wound yourself anymore? Again, it says: "Before we can approach the master, our feet have to be washed with the blood of the heart." That is, before you walk the path, you must wash your feet in love, which is the blood of the heart. Love means giving. Do you ever give away something you really want to keep, in the faith that this action is the only way it will ever really be yours? If you do, then you know something of love. And you must give away your negativities if you ever want them to be truly yours to profit from and outgrow.

FREE YOURSELF
FROM POSSESSIVENESS

Another thing we must do is drop the idea of stern possession, the feelings of "I" and "mine," and realize that everything we have is ours only by the grace of God. This does not necessarily mean that we are not allowed to have material possessions — hardly that. We are allowed to have all the material possessions in this world. All we can get is ours if we want it; but we should possess *it*, it should not possess *us*. Yet this is what happens so often; the it possesses the us. We are its slave. If you think this is not true, then just buy yourself a new house and fill it with new furniture. You will find yourself telling your children, "Don't sit on the chair! Watch it! That's new. I paid two hundred dollars for that chair!" We make palaces of our houses; we slave to get everything installed; and then we slave to keep it, making ourselves old by keeping the furniture new. It possesses us because we worked so hard for it. This is clearly backward. We should not constantly strive for possessions; they should come as fruits of our work, not as its goal.

Possessions also bring the fear that someone is going to take something from us. Strange. The only things that can be taken away from us are our perishables, the physical things that mean nothing. The only things we don't watch are our minds and our souls. We do not do anything to protect them from becoming clogged and their resources being lost to us. Instead, we protect those things we can touch and pick up with our hands or that we can put in our pockets. But these are only trinkets that can be lost, and shall be lost at death, if not sooner. But no one can ever take our convictions and our minds and our souls away. They can live forever. And they are worth some effort to protect, for their value can be lost to us if we do not cherish them.

"Seek ye first the kingdom of God and His righteousness and everything will be added unto you." All religious writings state this, but how many people know what it really means? If you see the godliness within yourself and start living it, you will own everything in this world and will not be owned by anything or anyone. You will be a free soul with a free choice and a free will. That is why you have to drop the ideas "I" and "mine."

LOVE YOUR AUSTERITY

Our material needs should be as simple as possible. We should obtain what we need spiritually and not long for material possessions. Those will come to us anyway as a product of our growth. The best possession we can have is austerity. Consider how highly our religions speak of fasting and praying. Consider why. Have you ever eaten a heavy meal and then had to go to work right away? Where is your thinking process then? Can you move easily? No, you want to drop into a chair; you have no energy and no thinking process left. This is why you fast and pray. It is true that food gives nutrition, but it also burns up energy as it is digested in your body. This takes energy away from your mental as well as physical processes. When you are fasting and praying, you do not get physical food, but you receive spiritual food, which is much more subtle and much more nutritious than physical food. Physical food is just a denser expression of what you receive through prayer. Through the subtlety of the spiritual food you receive by prayer, you operate more effectively. Of course, I like to change that word *prayer* to *meditation*. When you understand that in meditation you receive this particular inflow, you will realize that austerity is the best of all your possessions.

BE PATIENT

I hear people say, "If there is such a thing as a God, how can he allow suffering and killing and disease?" Who is allowing? God? God is doing it by man, through man, because man has not realized God within himself. This is the illness of the world. The ills of the world are man-made. This is why we are killing each other.

Of course, we can only kill the vehicles. We cannot actually kill anyone because the soul and mind still exist even though we kill the body. Nevertheless, we have no right to take those bodies. And it is we who are doing this and not God. It is because of humanity's lack of the realization of God that this is happening in the world. We must have trust in God; that is, we must have trust in ourselves and know that the universe was and is created perfectly. It is up to humans — to you — to keep it in its perfection. It is your heritage, your *only* heritage, to bring it back to perfection. Once you have done this, you will not need this clown suit we call the body. You can go in a little better style.

LEARN TO LOVE

Once we begin to guide our thoughts into a pattern of self-knowledge and refrain from thinking negatively about ourselves, we must also extend this to our thoughts of others. Thinking negatively about others is based on false knowledge. If we "feel" that person instead of looking at him, if we integrate ourselves with that person instead of considering him at the level of appearances, we might discover that he is a better being than we had thought. Become him for a little while by integrating with him through mental and spiritual intercourse; become sensitive to his feelings, to his vibrations. By experiencing them, not just by observing them, you will truly know who others are. And that will be an expression of your ability to love.

YOU HAVE MORE TO UNLEARN THAN YOU HAVE TO LEARN

Through our backgrounds and our educations, we have been forced into such rigid ways of thinking that we can hardly think for ourselves. We analyze too much and see too little. We lack the ability to become aware of our own inner knowing. Most of us are now so heavily conditioned that we accept only other people's authority. Quite often, for example, when I start a class, people come to me and say, "Should I follow this class?" I reply, "Well, you have to make up your own mind about that." Then they say, "Well, I've studied metaphysics for thirty years." Then I say, "Well, when are you going to start expressing it and practicing it?" Simply studying something, reading all the books in the world about it but never practicing or experiencing it, will not make you into an expression of the truth within the study. To become an expression of it is to transmute factual truth into living wisdom. What other purpose could there be?

Yet many people study metaphysics and get nowhere. Most of the time, such people are studying the phenomena of the world out of mere curiosity, and they are never capable of doing anything with themselves because they never discipline themselves to actualize the potentials within them that such study could stimulate. It is so easy, instead, to let the study, the learning, just go on and on. We have to realize that we have to do something about this. Instead of trying to learn so much, let us first start breaking down all the rules we have been taught and by which we analyze everything and catalog everything. Once we have thrown those rules away, we can begin to do something about ourselves.

Children are the fastest to learn and to unlearn. Fortunately, more and more parents are bringing their children to classes such as mine. These kids come up with questions so profound that adults are really shocked. They are *smarter* than we are not because they are more intelligent, but because they are not as inhibited. They are not as rigid in their thinking. They have fresh minds, they are keen observers, and they can involve themselves. They are not as inhibited as adults! My adult students come to my class saying, "Well, let's see what he is going to say tonight." Children just come in and listen, and they get the message.

Of course, you have to be skeptical of what I say; after all, I am only human, too. I think my ideas have come to me right out of the cosmos, and I obviously believe in them. But sometimes Jack Schwarz comes shining through, too, and distorts them. It should be your daily duty to jump up and say, "That isn't cosmic truth. That's Jack Schwarz off in the cloud bank." You should be capable of evaluating what I say (or what anyone says) in your mind, without harking back to some previous analytic conclusion that you learned from someone else.

ROUSE YOURSELF
FROM SPIRITUAL LETHARGY

Meditation is an act. It is active. It has its passive aspect, of course, which is more a state of being than a progressive action, but basically it is active. And what a time bomb you have on your hands! It is as powerful as all the creativity you possess. You can create something within two hours of meditation that you might never be able to do otherwise in your whole lifetime because meditation puts you in a place where you spend time with the creator within you.

To be sure, this does not usually happen all at once. At first many people sit a little while and then say, "Oh, no! This isn't for me; I'm just sitting here doing nothing. This is absurd, sitting here in silence." They do not realize that meditation is transforming them. Something is happening, even though they are not capable of seeing or feeling it. If they continue, they start feeling better. But they do not always know why they feel better; they sometimes get the idea that meditation is a miracle pill.

Let us realize that the powers released in meditation are active spiritual forces, forces that we can apply and use in our daily lives, and not merely forces that give us a passive feeling of exaltation. It is true that in the beginning stages this exaltation helps us to become more aware of our higher selves and our connection to the universe. But there are some dangers. First, our growth is in our awareness of the presence of the all-knowing; and at first, it is subtle, perhaps unnoticeable. This does not mean that it doesn't exist, that it isn't happening. We should not lose faith if, in the beginning, nothing seems to happen. Second, do not let the discipline become a habit, a mere pleasant routine, an automatic escape mechanism; let it always have a meaning and a higher purpose. And do not get drunk on it. When you become intoxicated with meditation, it easily becomes a method of escape, a way of withdrawal.

Let us also realize that spiritual forces, as we can experience them in our daily meditations, are at all times stronger than the forces that dwell in our subconscious minds. These subconscious forces are the accumulation of all our worldly physical experiences. The subconscious attempts to drive us; it urges us to follow its guidance exclusively. The power of the subconscious can drive a person without any consideration of direction or of spiritual goals. But we should not allow this to happen. We should nurture the spiritual forces so that their greater energy is free to propel us toward being, toward creativity, toward feeling that we are living souls expressing the prime substance, namely, spirit. It is through meditation that we can and should become aware of our spiritual qualities and goals. Only through the active, creative forces of the paraconscious mind, awakened in meditation, can transformation and growth take place.

What is the result of this awakening? We become polarized.

That is, we bring the positive and the negative into harmony within our hearts. The heart is the seat of consciousness, the place of atonement — that is, at-one-ment — in which one attunes oneself to the infinite, which is run through by the polarity of positive and negative. This atonement means to tune in to the infinite, to reflect its perfect order in our beings and our lives.

This may sound like a big order: to polarize all the forces by which you live (physical forces, mental forces, and spiritual forces) and to transform the cravings of the subconscious into the spiritual, liberating force of creativity. But it happens naturally because of the God-nature within you. All you do is absorb and resonate with the vibrations of universal divine mind. But first you have to waken these forces and shake them out of their state of dormancy. That means shaking yourself to get rid of your own lethargy, which has kept them dormant. You are a somnambulist, walking in your sleep. Your real self has yet to be discovered and experienced. You have to learn to open your eyes. Meditation is a beautiful path to this awakening.

Again, our children can be our teachers. Do not hesitate to invite them into your daily meditation. Because children have less unlearning to do, they can often help us remarkably with their insights. As a case in point, this happened when a doctor drew his two daughters into meditation. He found that he had never known them until he shared their experiences in meditation. They visualized red roses, full of energy and full of love; but when these two girls came out of meditation, they started to cry. Both parents asked, "Why are you crying?" The girls replied, "We saw beautiful red roses, but suddenly the petals started falling off, and they dried out. We looked down at our stems, and they withered away. Then we realized we were cut off at the roots." At that moment, the parents both realized that they were the roots and that the flowers, their children, were cut off from them. From then on, the whole family started to change. They talked their problems over together, and in general began to live together as a family. The two children had initiated this new order of living through their meditation. So never say that your children are too young to meditate. Maybe they are too old, and you are the one who is too young. Maybe they have already outgrown it and gone beyond you. You will only know the truths and the benefits that such experiences may bring if you try them.

Once we have opened our eyes, we can begin to absorb the incredibly rich contents of the universe. But we cannot stop there because we are more than just observers, we are beings engaged in life. Everything we absorb from the universe should be made into a mature image. Each of these mature images begins as an *idea potential*. Only through refinement of our own individualized minds will these potentials become manifest and find final expression in the outer world. It is important for us to activate the symbol or image, realizing it can be a seed thought. Seed thoughts are very important. As pure potential, they already have everything in them. That is the nature of the images or symbols we perceive in our creative meditations. It is what we perceive in the seven chakras when we see them as pictures with the seed syllables in them. Each seed syllable has the potential of a particular aspect of God. We should activate these seed thoughts and not just leave them as seeds. They are to be fertilized; they are to be nourished and given water so that they will grow and reach their potential. Like a plant, any idea potential has to mature. Then, just as this mature idea must grow a fruit, a physical expression, the images we receive in meditation must grow and be expressed.

When we have such a seed thought that needs nourishment, what do we feed it? We fertilize it with spiritual experiences and insights that we have experienced before, for these are stored away in our subconscious minds. And *how* do we feed it? By accepting it into our being; that is, by involution. Once, during meditation, a sentence came to me in the form of an anagram: "The creative act exists immediately in being." After meditation, the whole sentence reformed itself into this: "The creative act is the self-revelation of the powers of being." Being consists of the ability to create, and it is through being that creation reveals itself. We should understand that this creativity precedes all development. We have to plant seeds before we have any plants growing. The creative act is the seeding itself; that is awakened being. Furthermore, being has a twofold creative quality. First, there is the one, the God, and the original creator; second, there are the creations, which also have the power and being of creativity. If we observe the created world, we find that it was not only created but, through its innate nature, is also creative. We find the same qualities and aspects as those of the creator, God-within-man, who could thus be called a cocreator.

By recognizing this dual nature, we come to a better understanding of the Christian saying, "We were created in God's image." The nature of the divine creator is absolute and independent of time and the physical world. We are dependent on time and the physical world, but we are essentially creative to the exact extent that we have wakened to our cocreatorship. Because this wakening, this involution is itself a creative act, it precedes development, or evolution. Every potential power contained within the soul must become manifest in mind and express itself physically by the means of a creative act before it can evolve. We could say that the creative act is an addition to being. Thus, the individual soul finds its true existence in being, and once it has found that, its being develops in accordance with the cosmos. Only through this developing existence in being does the soul realize its bond with the cosmos. And once we have realized that we *are* the creative source (God), we cannot possibly deny the existence within ourselves of those qualities and aspects that we call divine. Such a denial could only lead to noncreativity and separation between humanity and God, between microcosm and macrocosm. Meditation, as we shall see, leads us in the opposite direction from this denial.

For too long, man's philosophy has been incomplete,

acknowledging only emanation as a power. But that does not suffice for an understanding of creativity. Through outflow, there is a loss of power; through constant creativity, there is a growth of power. When we look at the creative acts of God as described by all the world's religions, we find that by his creation of being, he added strength and power to himself. There was not a diminishing of power; rather, there was an increase. Power was also added by creating within this creation the ability to create, assuring thereby the constant inflow of power from the cocreative abilities of his absolute creation. In our philosophy we must recognize the powers of immanation, through which there is never a separateness between man and God, between macrocosm and microcosm. In doing this, we will attain the opportunity to manifest and to express our creativity. We will constantly be aware that spirituality must function consciously, actively, to add power to ourselves and to God through creative acts.

Rearrangement of existing substances cannot be called true creativity. Something that arises out of original substance contains the ability to increase the divine power of man; it is the only true creativity because these powers are immanent in us. We must understand that we can only reach the awareness of these powers by going through our individual, divine selves to find divine life, to find divine love. First we awaken from our state of lethargy and ignorance in which we have been searching in the outer world for signs or symbols of this innate power; then we realize that we should first search our inner world, using creative meditation as our vehicle. The goal is to absorb from the absolute power that particular substance that we require to fulfill our purpose as cocreators, adding power to ourselves, to the world, and to God. Now we realize that no outflow or emanation takes place without an inflow or immanation. We have gone within to receive what is there in order to create what does not yet exist.

I will give you an example of creativity and creative things. Have you ever found a fruit that does not have any seeds? In the same way, any fruit that you create through your creative acts has within itself the potentials of a creative act. If it were not so, we would not be progressive, would we? Any particular act that ends right there is not a creative act at all. When you were born, you carried seeds within you whereby someone can be born out of you. Jesus cursed the fig tree because it was barren of even one fig that could provide the seeds for new trees. This is why I keep putting emphasis on the creative act. If you stop acting and just start living on one vision you have had in your life, you are dead. You are a living-dead being because there is no creativity.

When you reach the age where you cannot work anymore, please become more creative. Bring meaning into your life. There are still seeds within you. Find them; grasp them; find meaning in life. Do not stop and say that you are going to retire. I retired fifteen years ago. I stopped working for money. Does that mean I'm working for free? No. But I stopped striving for it. I knew it would be there, the fruits of my creative acts. I would have seed money. If you want to grow, you have to have seeds and take care of them. Put them in fertile soil, not in sand. Also be sure to pick the chaff out of the wheat.

Remember, you are not just part of the universe. You are the total universe. You have a responsibility to nurture and actualize every seed within you, for your actions or lack of them affect everyone. They expand or constrict the cosmos itself.

four

MEDITATING CREATIVELY

It should be quite understandable now that transformation through creative meditation is not something we should attempt without preparation. We will have to reeducate our minds before we can transform them through the discipline of this process.

When the transmutation of the meditating mind into an aligned oneness has been achieved, it leads to complete integration. The mind manifests its state in a particular way of living through spiritually guided action. To make the transformation, we need to presuppose an ultimate purpose in the universe. Chapter 3 touched on this purpose. It is unity and harmony. After we have identified with this aim, we are left with a choice of many forms of meditative experience. Because we have to visualize our aims in order to identify ourselves completely with them, each of us should be like an archer who keeps an eye on the target to hit the mark with certainty. However, this mark, this complete unity and all-knowing oneness, has many aspects and hence is as immense and diverse to our conceiving minds as it is impressive in its unity, once we are able to perceive it in wholeness.

So we must look at each aspect as a target and realize that each is abstract and that, in meditation, these target aspects can only reveal themselves as symbols manifested to our senses. To let these symbols arise, we do not try to force any single thought into our minds. Rather, we wait very patiently for anything that comes, and very often our patience is rewarded. We then receive certain impressions, and we should trust them because we have allowed no desire to act in this process. They arise within our paraconscious minds when our rational conscious- ness is quiet. They are glimpses of the universe. It is true that we feel uplifted by them, but at this stage, they do not make a marked change in our lives.

We follow these symbols to discover the qualities of the nature of God, of ourselves. Being one within this nature does not necessarily make us aware of all its qualities. These aspects are initially presented to us as abstractions: God is love, God is truth, God is mercy, ad infinitum. But the only way we can really know what God is, is by experiencing these qualities, not by reading about them in books. Meditation is a method we can use to attain an experience of some of the aspects of God.

Creative meditation works on ideas. What you do is to pre- sent your mind with a theme and charge that idea with creative energy. To energize this theme, use a short, guided daydream or reverie. When you have achieved the result of that reverie, then propose this refined image of an idea as a theme and go into creative meditation. Use the same steps to carry yourself into both reverie and creative meditation. Later you will use them to carry yourself into passive meditation (which is the topic of the second part of this chapter) and then into the silence (which is the topic of Chapter 5).

To begin with, we choose a theme or a story. Using our imaginations, we create a three-dimensional scene outside of ourselves that portrays our theme. Then we create an image of ourselves that enters the scene and becomes part of it. For example, visualize a meadow, then a mirror image of yourself walking through this meadow. We decide consciously how and in what role our image joins the scene. The only conscious thought involved in meditation is directing this mirror image of ourselves. We never direct the scene itself; we just allow it to change and flow, as it will indeed do if we release our conscious attachment to it and let the unconscious express itself. Our conscious minds become the nonattached observers of the unfolding of the interaction of our mirror image and the changing theme. Throughout the unfolding, we remain aware and direct the mirror image to enter into aspects of the scene in different ways. This stimulates further release of imagery from the unconscious that we then can observe. What we observe in the mirror image is reflected within our own physical bodies and experienced there. This is very similar to becoming aware of emotions relating to the observing of a scene in a movie.

A reverie is not a theme, but the theme is hidden within it. The difference between creative meditation and reverie is this: In creative meditation, you do not change anything consciously; in a reverie, you sift and mix your anxieties and hopes, detecting their merits and possibilities at a glance.

Begin your practice of reverie and creative meditation with simple objects, and remember that you are seeking the experience of aspects of God within yourself. The simplest theme you can choose for either a creative meditation or a reverie is a common physical object, one that is easily visualized. Even though you think you are familiar with it, you will learn that you had hardly begun to experience its reality before meditating upon it.

There are many objects we can use for a beginning reverie; let us first choose a pink rose. We concentrate on the visualization of the pink rose. If it is easier, put a pink rose in front of you. Gaze upon the pink rose, contemplate it until you can feel yourself to *be* the pink rose. Feel the sap go through your stem and down your roots. Smell the scent of the flower; feel the vibration of the rose. Integrate into it completely. Become it. From then on, you will always remember you are a rose.

Or take a coffee cup, and see how it feels. Enter into its substance, and feel how it has to go through fire to be baked. Start with a ball of clay, create a cup within your inner mind, and see what it has to go through before you put it on your table and fill it with coffee. Now that cup is no longer just a physical, three-dimensional concept to you; it has become a living thing. This is the function of the reverie: to invest the theme with energy and to perceive the vitality and life within it. Then this theme becomes powerful enough to be the focus of your creative meditation.

Once we have become capable of doing this with physical objects, we should have little difficulty doing the same thing with the invisible abstracts, with the many aspects of God. Then we will know how to crystallize the symbols and visions belonging to that particular aspect because we will experience them.

You should not, for instance, be afraid to take an aspect of suffering as a topic for reverie. Even if you think you have not suffered much yet, it might be good for you to try this topic; you will understand more clearly why your fellowman is hurting so much. In Gibran's *The Prophet*, the woman says to the master, "Speak to me of joy." He answers, "Your joy of today is your suffering of yesterday unmasked." That is exactly it; you cannot know the one unless you know the other; you have to know both aspects. Therefore, do not hesitate to meditate creatively upon the painful. Integrate into your meditation a few things that you think are negative and that you would rather not go through in life. Isn't it much better to go through them in meditation, so that if they come to you, you will already be acquainted with them? Then you will know what to do with them, for you will have felt and lived through the experiences they symbolize.

The formal steps to reverie and creative meditation are concentration, decentration, contemplation, synthesis, and erasure.

Our first step is to concentrate on the theme of a story or an idea. To do this, we envision a three-dimensional scene. The second step is what we call decentration. We create a mirror image of ourselves to enter and interact with some aspect of the scene while we ourselves remain outside as observers. This interaction is called penetration into the theme. In this aspect of meditation, *we direct our mirror image,* thereby psi-phoning from the cosmos through our unconscious. This method is like siphoning gas from one tank to another. The paraconscious mind is like the main tank out of which all knowledge comes. Our conscious minds are usually out of contact with that source because they are blocked by fears, desires, anxieties. In meditation, we want to draw some of this knowing into our conscious perceptions. To siphon gas, an initial force or suction must be applied to one end of the hose to draw the liquid from the other end. This is our purpose when we consciously direct our mirror image to interact with the scene. In the same way that the gas then flows freely without further force, the intuitive energy flows into and changes the scene after being stimulated by the action of our mirror image.

To gain the benefits of this energy, we must allow it to flow without intervention from the rational mind. If the rational mind becomes active, do not let it interfere with your observation. Let the train of thoughts pass you by, as though you are waiting for a train to go by so that you can cross the tracks. Maintain your nonattached state; remember that your purpose is to cross the tracks, not to catch a train. Do not try to expel or force the train of thoughts. If you do, you will become attached to them, and the intuitive flow will stop. The second image should let the train of thoughts pass and then proceed to penetrate the scene, becoming one with it without changing it.

At this point, the third step, contemplation, begins. Your conscious mind maintains a nonattached state to absorb fully all that it observes during the penetration. Here you begin to recall and recollect what is happening in a passive way. This implies that you must recognize your own ability to perceive clearly what is arising from the paraconscious. You do not need to have it verified by anyone else because you are aware that anyone else can only verify it from his or her own individual perspective.

For the fourth step, we synthesize; we put it all together. We do not become involved, for that would carry us toward attachment, and we need not become involved with details anymore. To be sure, we have observed all the details in a state of passive volition, and recorded them in our minds, but it is not with details that we work at this stage. We have been looking at the trees. Now it is time to start looking at the forest, to know the totality again. In synthesizing, you mentally surround your vision with energy so that you place it in a totality. I find that the easiest way for me to energize it is literally to throw light on it. Mentally, I shine white light on it, framing it so that it becomes more visible to me. Then I erase the image and let it melt. Actually, I let it integrate with everything by putting in more energy so that it starts to dissolve into everything that is.

The process is the same for reverie and for creative meditation. The difference between the two is that in creative meditation, no further conscious direction is made after the first psi-phoning; whereas in reverie, we continue to draw or psi-phon from the paraconscious. We instruct and guide our mirror image to experience fully and merge with all aspects of the reverie. In this way, we energize our theme so that it is a provocative focus for a creative meditation.

In meditation, what you see, feel, and hear seem to be physical experiences. Be aware that you are really experiencing the inner world by means of your inner senses. Each of us will experience these sensations in different ways, according to our own needs and development. Some of us might see visions in black and white; others, in color. We know that there are animals who see only in black and white; they cannot recognize colors. But they have a greatly developed sense of smell; they also have a much greater sense of hearing than we have. Pigeons, on the other hand, see at least ten times more color in one shade than we can.

To me, it is not important what color you see. What is more important is that you *see,* for these experiences are very valuable. They should become active spiritual forces that can be applied and utilized in your daily life, instead of being just pleasant feelings, passive exaltation.

In creative meditation, symbols of this inner world will serve as catalysts with the power to transform the invisibles into the visibles. It is like the crystallization of a liquid. It is a productive meditation, a process of creative enfoldment. However, let us not allow these crystallized images to stay in their solid form; through integration, let us make them subtle again.

What do I mean by that? By absorption, by resonance, by tuning into the vibrations of the subtle forces that form pictures in your mind, they solidify like a liquid becoming a solid; they crystallize. But how much room do you have to put all those solids within yourself? You will have to activate that particular picture. It should become a form of power, of creative action, through even higher vibrations. Break down that crystallization. You have to turn it into a practical application, using high vibrations of love so that it dissolves into subtle forces again. This is the process of alchemical transformation, making the subtle concrete and then subtle again. It is the word becoming flesh that it may become aware of itself and be transmuted back into light. Let it shine through your acts.

A perfect act is a physical expression of the mental manifestation of this spiritual integration. But unless that integration is carried through to the physical level, it will remain an unfertilized seed. And it is very easy to become attached to the visions we have observed in silence. Very often we do not realize that a revelation is not the apex of experience, that it is just the seed needing to mature by being allowed to grow into a perfect act. Your visions should pass through this stage and become action. Do not gaze at one vision for a lifetime. Otherwise, when the curtain falls and the stage becomes invisible again, you will not know how to act.

Eventually, the visions should come ten times, twenty times, a thousand times a day. The goal is for meditation no longer to be limited to certain times. Meditation will become action, action will be meditation, and you will have continuity. It will be as if you had rented all the movies in the world, as if you had become a living movie screen. Once you have learned creative meditation, these movies will keep on going, day in and day out. Without ever stopping, you will have creative inspirations and intuitive power flowing through you. They will run on if you are aware, and you will act on and react to them. This is what real creative meditation is all about.

It does not mean that when this happens you do not have to discipline yourself anymore or that you can quit meditation. You might have to "discuss" the scripting of your meditations with the universe through the paraconscious from time to time. You may have the ideas, but it is better to listen to the authority of the inner voice and the inner vision so that you do not start acting by yourself. You must still realize where the power comes from, and this realization can be reached through meditation. Discipline is what keeps you close to the source of this divine power. It is important to remember this every day; otherwise, you might think that you are just leasing it temporarily. It is best, as it were, to call on your boss, let him know what you are doing, and show him your income and expenditures.

It is important that you do not let the vision remain just a mental manifestation. Acknowledge its truth, and act on it. Do not fear it or try to control it consciously. Just let it happen; let it ripen; then express it. The active expression of truth is the purpose of life. Actions based on truth bring us more and more in tune with the universe, establishing us all in a better relationship with it. This kind of action is our aim in meditation.

Learn to know the difference between creative imagination and conscious imagination. A blind patient, with whom I worked closely for over a year, once confessed to me, "The day I lost my eyesight was the day I started to see." We are so distracted by what our eyes show us that we don't listen to what our ears or our feelings tell us. So, if we take seeing too literally, we cut off the other experiences we can have with the other senses. It's fine if you get a picture, but if you get it in feeling or in sound or through another sense, that's fine, too. You may have to experience many meditations before you really understand the meaning of the sounds, the visions, the symbols, the colors you have perceived. Actually, you should recognize your vision to be only one expression of what you receive through meditation.

We must not confuse these experiences with the ones that we consciously create or with the dreams that we arouse during our sleep as the result of fear, anxiety, and wishful thoughts. With my conscious mind, I can produce any vision on a blank wall. For example, I can gaze for ten minutes and project a circle on it. I am quite sure that I will see the circle; that is conscious imagination. But if I am standing and talking to you and suddenly I turn around and see a circle on the wall, then I know my conscious mind had nothing to do with it. Certain visions or experiences that we go through we could call our cosmic picture gallery. They come mostly during meditation, after meditation, after purification, after the emptying of our minds, or in our sleep as an inspirational dream or a dream that shows you the path that you will have to follow.

The visions that we perceive during meditation will settle in our creative growth centers. Even if they are not used at the moment, they will settle down there and ripen like seeds until the proper time. That they are only seeds or seedlings is of course the product of our lack of awareness. If we had awareness when they came in and settled down, we could have used them right then and there. But we lacked the awareness, or we were not in a state of hyperperception. So new thoughts and meditations, new energies, come in and add nourishment to the dormant seedlings, which are very potent; and we finally break them open, and awareness takes place. Meditation gives us guidance and opportunities to ripen the seeds and throw off the fruits in physical expression and action.

This entire meditation process can easily fill up two hours, but I would not advise anyone to start with two hours. I would start with a shorter time: five minutes washing out, five minutes for stating your problems and your confirmations, followed by fifteen minutes of the exercise with the theme, and ending with fifteen minutes in the silence. After you have been able to do this a number of times, add fifteen minutes more to the silence. You do not need to add to the other steps; add only to the silence in the beginning.

In my own practice, I use three minutes for the affirmations and three to ten minutes for the washing out, or a total of about fifteen minutes for the washing out and the confirmations, then two hours in the silence. I would not suggest this for others, any more than I would suggest my own diet to others because it probably would not work for them. Because you are trying to attain full self-awareness, it is important that you adapt any technique or practice to your individuality, that you let your individuality form your path.

The two hours that I spend in the silence are really for feeding the spirit, the mind, the body by concentrating on bringing in spiritual power. That is all that you need to feed upon in this life. It is all the same substance; the creative power and that which you find on your dish, this nutrition from plants and animals. The animals find it in the plant. Plants find it in the soil of the earth and in the light of the sun. All these are just passing forms of spirit, solidified into the lower vibration of this planet. Why not go right to the wholesale dealer and get it from the universe? Why go through all these retailers? We must realize that there are many grades in the school of life. Those who are in kindergarten and nursery school will have to get nutrition from forms of spirit at their own levels of vibration, from the plants and animals. Later on, we may evolve so that we can draw directly from the creative source itself for our nourishment.

It sounds like some kind of maze, doesn't it. Yet it is all just the process of growing. You know how silly we really are, but we have to have this silliness in order to grow. But it is really such a waste! Just imagine the hours people spend in buying, eating, preparing, digesting, getting dishes done afterward, and all the hours sleeping. You tire your body out by going to sleep. It is true. If you washed yourself out by screening your mind every day, you could within a week reduce your need for sleep to only seven hours a night instead of eight. After a couple of weeks, six hours would be sufficient. From your meditation you could achieve so much emptying out that after a while you would hardly need to sleep at all. Sleep should be used to revitalize your body and still your mind. Yet just the opposite happens; people are more tired when they get up than they were when they went to bed.

Creative meditation involves an emphasis on conscious actions. Penetration is a conscious action. Contemplation is a conscious action. Synthesizing is a conscious action. You are consciously involved in awakening that unconscious. And you will be stirring yourself up. I have spoken to many meditators who followed specific methods of meditation for two or three months, and everything seemed to be going along fine. Then their meditations began to produce all kinds of problems, including mental obstacles. These even resulted in very destructive feelings, feelings of resentment and of hate. What was actually happening was just the result of three months of stirring up their own subconsciouses. This world is like a pond left standing for a little while. When you leave it alone and look at it, it is still and clear; but when you stir it, all kinds of sediment and residue come to the surface. For many years, you have never really cleaned out your house; you have been shoveling dirt under the rug. And as long as you didn't see it, it wasn't there. You have lived happily until now, until today, when you have to lift the rug up. And now you will probably find yourself sinking into the stuff you have been sweeping under the rug.

Meditation should put a stop to that type of dirty living, but it means that you have to deal with your past. It is much better if you become a bit more of a spiritual housekeeper, who every day cleans the dishes out of the sink and puts the clothing away and keeps everything clean. Then the next day you only need to spend a little time in maintaining it that way.

On the other hand, many people in meditation have seen their whole lives being changed and their problems being solved. There is no reason why meditation should not become a problem solver. But how do we do it?

In the first place, never think about problems and mull them over during these periods. So long as you keep thinking and talking to your inner mind, you cannot hear what the inner self wants you to hear. It is that simple. You are like a radio set, transmitting and receiving. If you start transmitting and receiving at the same time, you will get nothing but discord and gibberish. You will not be able to understand; you will not be tuned in properly and will not be able to communicate.

If you *do* have something troubling you, you should cleanse yourself, through a state of concentration and contemplation, before meditation. State your problems in an affirmative way, with no wailing and weeping. State it firmly: "This is my problem." Do not be like the man who said to me, "I have no problems." I told him, "Your problem is that you have not recognized your problems."

Never feel bad about your problems. At all times, recognize this important fact: The universe has polarity. As soon as a problem is created by you or by your environment, at the very moment that the problem is created, a solution for the problem is also created. Every coin, even the coin of your problem, has two sides.

If you keep staring at the problem, it will become so severing that you will not be able to see the solution, which lies just on the other side. You will be telling yourself that you are looking for a solution, but you will be lying to yourself. If you were, you would not be looking at the problem anymore.

So state the problem for what it is, and then push it aside. Put it on the left side of your mental accounting book, as an expenditure. Look to see how you can profit by it. You will need to take some time for looking at the solution. Notice that I said "looking *at* the solution," not "looking *for* the solution." The solution is right there; you just have to turn your consciousness to it. Let it come to you. If it does not come to you at first, state your problem again in the next meditation period. That is how meditation can become the dissolver of your problems. It shows you the solutions. But you must allow it to happen.

After learning to meditate creatively, we are prepared to begin passive meditation. In Chapter 5, we shall go into the topic of passive meditation in detail. Here, since we are just concerned with preparing ourselves for that silence, we need to understand only one fact: The outcome of your creative meditation returns to you in passive meditation, automatically, in more positive form. That is, the passive state recalls the outcome without involving the conscious mind. Thus, what we have developed during the creative phase is resolved during the passive phase.

By passive meditation, I mean going into the silence, which is not just to sit in silence after erasing the themes on which you concentrated in creative meditation. Rather it means to summon and use your energy for action. Therefore, we must prepare our minds and bodies to direct that energy. To prepare ourselves for passive meditation, we must build the feeling that we have accomplished purification, contemplation, and affirmation of the unity in the universe. All I am saying, actually, is that we must affirm ourselves. Now, to prepare ourselves to go within, there are some exercises we can use to polish the accomplishments we have achieved in creative meditation.

In the first exercise, contemplate a candle, and meditate on it as a symbolic representation of yourself. Sit up straight, spine erect, neck properly aligned with the spine. If you are in a group, don't cross your legs, and don't touch your hands. Instead, rest them, palms up, in a relaxed way on your lap or knees. If you are alone, cross your legs in a lotus or half-lotus position if you can and put your hands on top of each other, letting the thumbs touch each other. Why? If you are alone, you don't want to dissipate your energy, so you can close your circuits by crossing your arms and legs. But in a group situation, you will want to share your energy with the others in order to create a group consciousness. So sit up straight, and gaze into a candle flame. The candle flame is the symbol of light, weaving, bobbing, and trying to reach the apex of its own being. Let this be symbolic to us as we realize that we, too, are sources of light.

Contemplation is a part of the exercise. We go into the exercise of contemplation of the candle by looking at all the aspects of the candle. In the same manner, some Buddhist traditions advise practitioners to contemplate the navel as a point of concentration. They recognize the navel as the symbolic connection to their source. What this means is that though we appear to be separate beings, we are actually connected to the universe. When we focus on the candle, we recognize that the light within us is our connection to the absolute enlightened state, which is both our source and our goal. Again, here we are using the preparatory exercises of concentration and decentration. Our minds become focused, and we become aware of our relationship to our paraconscious minds.

At this initial stage, we use the candle as the theme and contemplate its meaning to us. It is analogous to a human being — to you, for instance. The candle is made of wax, a moldable substance. When you light the wick, energy is released from the wax into this spine in the candle. At the same time, oxygen is drawn from the atmosphere and merges with the matter of the wax, and a transmutation takes place that creates a visible flame. When you go into meditation, you release energy out of your body that flows into your wick, your spine. At the same time, you attract, by resonance, the etheric energy that always surrounds you. This merges with the released energy collected in your spine to create your inner light. Just because you may not physically see your flame doesn't mean that it isn't there.

Now if you were to cut off the energy from the solid matter and keep only the oxygen, your flame would go out. And, of course, fire cannnot exist without oxygen either. So the two energies — the energy from above and the energy from below — are required.

Another lesson can be learned from the fact that the wax melts and flows freely when the flame grows hot. Its substance becomes more subtle, and it expands. When your inner flame increases during meditation, it melts away the rational form of your perceptions, revealing the flowing, intuitive resources and powers within you. The flame is actually a representation of you; the dark spot at the core of the flame is like that pilot light at your center whose concentrated heat gives brighter light as it vibrates higher.

As you contemplate the candle, think about the wick being the spine of the candle, drawing its energy from the base of the candle, as you are doing from the base of your spine. Then think about the soft, melting wax that is forming a pool around the wick, and realize that you would love to become as fluid and pliable as that wax so that your thoughts will not be as rigid as they have been. Let this become a symbol for you. Then see that the color of the candle is burning away through the flame. When the wax begins to melt, the color starts disappearing from the middle of the candle, which becomes pure white. Isn't that a beautiful symbol of burning your soul into purity? What more perfect symbol could you have before you? The representation of yourself. Think about the flame of life, the flame of light, the flame of truth. Soon this fiery flow will carry you beyond thought to the fullness of the void within.

As a second exercise, contemplate the flame, and meditate on its symbolic meaning for you. Here we are going to develop an ability called *contemplative fixation,* in which we focus our minds upon a single object and thereby both lose the awareness of our conscious minds and arrest the aimless wanderings of this part of our minds. Put a lighted candle on a table about six to eight feet away from where you are sitting, making sure the candle is at about eye level. Gaze into the flame with open eyes at first, for about thirty seconds to one minute. When your fixation has been established properly, you should not see anything in the room except the flame of the candle. With practice, this entire exercise can be done in your imagination with no physical props, not even a candle.

Now let thoughts about the candle come into your mind. Remember that this flame represents your pilot light, which is rising and will reach higher and higher toward your apex, your highest center. The next step can also be done either with a tangible, physical candle or with an imaginary, mental candle. Squint your eyes (or imagine doing this) by gently letting your eyelids drop until they are nearly closed, but do not lose your fixation on the candle. Then you'll see the candle's rays ascending and descending in all directions. At a certain limit, they are cut off. Does that mean that they don't exist anymore? It only means that they have surpassed your visible field. But they continue to exist. As a matter of fact, the rays will touch everything there is and will ultimately return to their source, their cause. So you, like the candle, send out your flames of spirit, whose rays will resonate with all there is and eventually return to their source, you.

Your expanding light brings you into contact with things of which you are not normally aware. These are like strings that connect you with the cosmos. Follow one of these rays, and see where it takes you. Then, think that these rays are going to bring light to the dark paths of some of your fellow human beings, that your ray of light might enlighten them and take the shadows of doubt out of their being. Because where there is light, there can be no darkness under any circumstances. This, too, is the symbol of the candle. If you momentarily bend your head slightly forward, you will see a bundle of rays directed straight at your heart, and you may have a physical reaction there. Even if you only visualize and follow one of these rays, you will achieve a feeling of expansion as you become more and more nonattached. Very soon, you will not be aware of your physical environment. I know it is just your imagination. Thank God for that. The only creative force in the whole cosmos *is* imagination. Let these rays of light become a key that opens your heart. Let them become the arrows that pierce the heart; let your heart become the target and the rays of light the arrows that pierce it. Then you can wash your feet with the blood of the heart.

As a third exercise, pass from the candle to your own inner light. Trace it, encase yourself in it, accelerate it. Close your eyes and create the mental image of a candle already flaming. Remember that the candle is a good model of your own being. As the candle releases energy out of its physical wax into the wick, this wick at the same time draws energy out of the atmosphere. When this process occurs, it creates the visible flame. You, too, will release energy out of your physical substance into your wick, your spine, and draw energy from the immaterial ethers to create your visible flame. At the same time that this is happening, the wax is melting, becoming a flow of flexible substance. It is expanding and becoming more transparent. So you allow yourself to become more moldable, more flexible, and more transparent. Become aware of the rays of light that radiate from the flame to all the directions of the universe. Become aware of your intuitive flame radiating into the cosmos, attached by rays of light to all that exists. Light resonates back to you and releases new energies.

Now, move your attention to the center of your forehead, and look up and backward into your cerebral area. When you do this, you will experience a tiny spot of light. Some people will feel it, and some may see it. By focusing on this pilot light, you enable its energy to rise along the spine toward the brain, and you will feel its warmth. I suggest this so that you can grow familiar with your untapped energy.

Look up, as if you had your finger on the middle of your forehead and you were looking at your finger. Raise your eyeballs as high as possible and look back into your cranial area. Allow yourself to experience a tiny spot of light. It will seem as though you are looking through a cylinder at the end of which you see the light. The light is very concentrated, very bright; it is the image of your own pilot light at the sacral area of your spine, reflected by the pituitary gland, which functions as the mirror bringing the light to the spiritual eye. Imagine yourself moving through this cylinder toward the light, and observe the physiological action that takes place. When you reach the end of this cylinder, it will be as if you are filled with the energy of this light.

As soon as this occurs, throw the light forward from your forehead as if you were wearing a mine worker's helmet with a floodlight; flood the whole environment with the light. Don't give it direction; just allow it to be released. As it surrounds you, it will form a protective shield around you, blocking the passage of any lower energy patterns. You will suddenly see your whole head being filled with light. You are filling your entire environment with light. It permeates you until inwardly and outwardly you *are* light. You are accelerating this light until it becomes a blinding, bright, pure, clear, radiant light. Allow it to exist, and pay attention to it no more.

This is the third step of meditation on the candle. Now you will want to expand yourself and accelerate this light, and you will start vibrating higher. Then you will give this light to the universe.

Passive meditation also requires that you breathe carefully and properly. We must guide and direct breath properly through the body so that we receive the ultimate nourishment from it.

The first act is to take a deep breath with your diaphragm, not with your lungs. For many women, this will not be too hard because when they give birth to children, they have to learn to breathe with their diaphragms. Hold the air in your abdominal area, fill your abdominal area with breath, but do not take in so much that you are a balloon. Take just what is comfortable for you, but fill yourself up so there will be just a slight pressure. Hold this breath in, and then release it with a sigh. Then hold

your breath out. You might begin with eight seconds of holding, but later you will be capable of longer control. Do this
twice.

1. Inhale through your nostrils, filling your diaphragm and
   your chest and hold it in for eight seconds. However, do not
   concentrate on counting; keep your attention on the proper
   breathing. Exhale.
2. Then inhale again, and, holding the air in your abdominal
   area, press one nostril closed with your index finger. Hold
   your breath in. Then exhale through the open nostril,
   making certain that all the air is expelled. You can correlate
   this mentally with the image of all your problems being
   expelled with that air. You get rid of all the foul air; at the
   same time, you rid yourself of all your problems. Thus you
   make room for finer particles instead of coarser particles.
3. Put your hand down, and inhale through both nostrils,
   filling your abdomen.
4. With your other index finger, close the other nostril. Then
   exhale through the open nostril. Repeat these four steps a
   few more times. Then drop your hands back into your lap.
5. Now inhale with both nostrils again, deeply; hold it in,
   longer this time; and release it with a sigh. Hold it out
   longer this time. Inhale deeply, hold it in, and just let it go.

I must warn you that you might create a vacuum on one side
of your body and suddenly feel a snap in your forehead. It
might be something like feeling your ears pop as you ascend in
an elevator. Don't worry about this; it is just the clearing of a
sinus. When you create a vacuum, a little membrane will relax
or have a little pressure exerted upon it; that is the snapping.
Do not let this feeling or sound disturb you.

To increase the effect of this deep breathing exercise, go
through the first four steps twice more. Hold the breath longer
this time, for fifteen seconds if possible, both on inhalation and
exhalation. Each time, let the breath go with a sigh so that you
will feel completely relaxed. I always have a hard time when I

guide students through this. They tend to float away. Even the sounds of these exercises make one feel more comfortable.

After completing the sequence, just let go of your breathing. Your subconscious mind will eventually take over and maintain your breathing in a regular rhythm. Do not pay any more attention to your breathing.

Finally, use autogenic relaxation techniques to prepare yourself for the silence within. We use autogenic relaxation exercises because they quiet our physical bodies so that we lose our awareness of them. As long as your body still stirs, aches, itches, or whatever, you obviously cannot enter silence. These exercises have been found very useful for that purpose.

Some people who have meditated several times and then followed my classes have said, "Jack, there's one thing wrong with the meditation. During the relaxation exercises, I fall asleep." I have answered, "Oh, shouldn't you? Well, if your body wants to fall asleep, let it. But your mind should stay alert." Thus, part of autogenic suggestion is the phrase "mentally we stay alert." One time I forgot to say this. It was in Los Angeles, and I had twenty-eight people sitting in the audience. During the meditation, I forgot to say, "Mentally you stay awake," and I had twenty-eight sleeping people on my hands. I had to wake them all up before we could continue the meditation.

Now, repeat to yourself, mentally, without a sound: My forehead is cool; my solar plexus is warm. It is most important to have the right intonation. (The French say, "C'est le ton qui fait la musique" — it is the tone that makes the music.) If I say, "My forehead is cool" in a slow, grumbling way, the tone does not give a very good effect, does it? Or, if I say coldly and quickly, "My solar plexus is warm," that doesn't give a very good effect either. So I must say this in the manner in which I feel it. I say it slowly and with feeling and meaning so that I know I have become what my words describe. The first thing we always say is: "I am at peace." Then we quietly speak aloud these phrases:

I am at peace. My forehead is cool; my solar plexus is warm. My arms and legs are heavy and warm.

Repeat this three times, and the last time be sure to add:

But mentally I am alert. Spiritually I am awake.

Then you say:

I am at peace, my forehead cool, solar plexus warm, my heartbeat calm and regular. And my arms and legs are so heavy and so warm, but mentally I am alert, and spiritually I am awake.

Then:

I am at peace. I am completely relaxed in body, mind, and soul, and now I can go within.

Then:

I am completely relaxed in body, mind, and soul, and now I go within the silence.

Now the silent period begins. We have reached the level of being completely prepared to go within the silence. Our conscious minds are no longer interfering. Our breathing is calm and deep, and our bodies are quiet, no longer disturbing us. We are ready to enter our mysterious inner selves, to see, hear, smell, taste, touch, and experience whatever they desire to reveal. The revelations all depend on our level of growth. In most instances in which this technique has been used, signs of development appear very quickly. Most important in meditation is the ability to visualize and to experience its awareness in all aspects of life. All senses are filled, even your psychic senses, for that is what should happen.

five

ENTERING THE SILENCE
BEYOND ALL SOUND

Let me first give you a quick sketch of what will happen when you go into the silence. To begin with, you will see all kinds of little flashes of light, colors, sometimes stars or diamonds, all types of geometric figures. Next, you will see the colors flowing together, becoming waves of light and color. Sometimes they start to form pictures.

Somewhat later, the theme revealed during reverie will come into action. Remember that choosing it was one of the preparations for meditation. You selected one quality or abstraction on which to focus. You wanted to know truth, and that means learning about all its aspects. It is very difficult to perceive the aspects because they are abstracts, known through intuition, not through logical verification. Faith, adherence, being, discipline, beauty, charity, love, humility, patience, resignation, persistence, aspiration, peace, joy, forgiveness, gratitude, suffering, goodness, health, holiness, salvation — all these are intangibles. How can you get to know about them, experience them, feel them? This was your original starting point, although you may have phrased it differently to yourself.

So before you went into meditation, you said, "Today, I choose patience as an abstract." Or "today, as an abstract, I take peace." During your creative meditation, if it was centered on peace, you may have seen a bird, a white dove flying around with a small twig in his beak; then you should have known that your conscious mind was still giving you a conscious symbol of peace. You probably have actually experienced something entirely different from the most common physical symbol, and this is good. We must allow the symbolism of our own being to arise from within. And if you allowed a symbol to rise from your paraconscious — it might have been a tranquil well or whatever — and meditated on it with honest creativity, then it is the outcome of that meditation that will come flashing back to you here in the silence.

So it follows that the passive aspect of meditation depends for its effectiveness on the preceding stages of creative meditation. With this sufficient preparation and its revelation of our own symbols for our chosen themes, we can go on to discuss the silence in broader terms.

BE SENSITIVE TO THE
FORCES YOU MEET

Our physical senses are able to grasp only a small fraction of the range of possible vibratory rates. John Tyndall (1820–1893), a British scientist interested in heat, sound, and light, predicted that humanity would be able to learn to perceive and utilize vibrations of all conceivable and inconceivable kinds. At present, we are discovering many of those vibrations and are starting to use them to our benefit. We are capable of being anything we perceive—not what we wish to be, but what we perceive, for everything we perceive is, in a certain sense, part of our own beings.

You are the universe, and the universe is filled with these forces. Anything you perceive from this universe is part of your own being. Therefore, you have the potential to comprehend, to merge with the entire universe, but you can achieve this only by becoming conscious of all its aspects. Every force of the universe is capable of being transformed or transmuted into any other kind of a force or form. You should understand that there is always an inexhaustible supply of these forces when you need them; you just have to learn how to draw them to yourself and absorb them by resonance. For example, water is transformed into electricity; heat, into light; sound, into music; and music, into words.

In particular, we can use the vibrations of sound for creative purposes, as well as for destructive purposes. Of course, humans do not have the true power of destruction. We can only change the form and shape of a substance. We cannot destroy, regardless of how much we shatter, for even that which is shattered remains in the universe.

We can use universal forces in only two ways: for positive purposes or for negative purposes. The positive is to serve humankind, and the negative is to destroy humankind. This is the law of polarity; where there are positive forces, there have to be negative forces. Just as the magnet has two poles, a negative one that attracts and a positive one that repels, so all of material existence is governed by this law. In physics, nuclear particles have a charge, either negative or positive. It is the interaction of all these charges that are perceived as physical events.

This law applies to nonphysical events as well. Our crises result from these forces not being in harmony. When they are in balance, the rhythm of life is restored. But we tend to use either too much positive or too much negative. Too many positive forces are as bad as too many negative forces. Remember that I am not talking about good and bad. Those are the connotations that humans have given these forces. What is essential to growth and evolution is the perception of all the forces of the universe, whether they are in their positive or their negative aspect. By using the catalyst of acknowledging the divine order, we can transmute all aspects into a totally

creative concept. A creative concept means a concept in balance, having equal polarities: 50 percent negative and 50 percent positive. Your perceptions will then be on the fulcrum of
your being and will balance out. You are in rhythm; the pendulum is swinging smoothly left to right and right to left. It is
balance we seek to reach.

Each of us should understand that we *are* the universe, not
just a part of it. Therefore, we are meant to become perfect
conducting instruments, channels free of obstructions, instead
of insulating ourselves. How do we insulate ourselves? By
separating ourselves from the universe and not understanding
that we are the universe. Separateness is insulation. If I separate myself from you, I do not feel you anymore. I can insulate
myself against all your vibrations, regardless of how good they
are. But I cannot separate myself from you if I want to know
what you are and who you are. To know anyone or anything, I
must become one with it, experience as it experiences, acknowledge it to be part of me.

It is important to understand that we can employ only those
forces that we are able to embrace with complete understanding. This depends, of course, on our own mental capacity and
level of perception, for we all progress from different levels
and in different manners. As I mentioned before, some of us
are in nursery school, and some of us are in kindergarten,
learning the alphabet. One of these days we might go to
elementary school and all start learning how to put the letters
together. If we really understand that we are on different
levels, we will not judge or evaluate anyone on another level.
When I hear people say, "But I can't have him in my class; he
isn't ready yet," I wonder what they mean. The student might
be more ready than we think, maybe even more developed
than we are. We can only judge the person on our own level; it
takes one to know one. We cannot know anything beyond that
level because we have not yet experienced the next level and we
should have forgotten the level below.

The extent of our relationship to the universe is limitless.
This fact is clouded from us because we tend to bind ourselves

up with certain rigid forms of thought; we get caught up in one or another kind of analytic measurement, analytic thinking. But this is unnecessary. To utilize the universal powers or forces, we need to understand that each of us is limited by only one factor: the level of our own consciousness. If we know this, then we must do something with this level of consciousness: namely, raise it by perceiving more of the universe. We grow in this way, step by step. The more we grow spiritually, the more forces we are able to attract and apply.

Essentially, you are sufficient unto yourself. However, you will be very unsatisfactory to yourself until you have reached a complete and unconditional harmony and relationship with the universe. You have experienced only a few of the many aspects of spirit. To name one, most of us have experienced a quality or aspect of love. Because I do not wish to judge and evaluate, I can only look at my own life and say, yes, to a certain degree I have experienced that. But as for the totality of love, well, I am still trying to reach that apex. Ask yourself how far you have reached the understanding of love or of any of the nonphysical forces that rule the world of experience.

You perceive only a few of these forces and probably only in their grosser aspects. Try to perceive their more subtle vibrations. To improve our rapport with the universal forces, we can tune into vibrations beyond the normal perceptual capabilities of our physical senses. Many experiments show that this is possible. Today in Bombay, Professor Vinod is conducting experiments with people who were born blind and are enabled to see through meditation.* After meditation, he places a microscope on their cheeks, and they are able to describe in detail what they see in the microscope. I also know of a boy whose vision was poor and deteriorating. Finally, one eye had to be replaced with a glass eye. His mother took him to an evangeli-

---

*Professor Vinod has been doing research under the auspices of the Department of Parapsychology of the Indian Government (Dr. H. N. Banerjee, Director). This information was related to me by a friend after he visited India.

cal healing session. The boy went forward, but the healer did not notice that he had a glass eye. He told him he would see through both eyes, and his eyesight would be perfect: "God is healing you now, and you will see with both eyes; you will see perfectly." Then the healer slapped the boy on the shoulder. Three months later, the boy could see perfectly from his good eye. When tests were taken and he closed the good eye, the boy could also see with his glass eye. Of course, you realize the boy was not looking through his glass eye at all. He had the ability to see through something that was not even there. This teaches us that the physical instrument of vision, the eye, is not the only means by which we can see.

Some deaf people can hear music by just placing an instrument upon their bodies. It doesn't matter where the instrument is placed — on the forehead, on the back, on the soles of the feet, on the palms of the hands. They hear through vibrations in a much better way than we can hear, for our ears are still absorbing other noises that mingle in with music. Deaf people do not have that trouble. They hear music in its purest form by receiving only these musical vibrations through their bodies.

Now, depending on the circumstances, we can become more perceptive and increasingly able to perceive by more means. When I speak of circumstances, I mean the conditioning of the self as well as the arrangement of the conditions of the environment. We are able to attract any force to our being, to achieve any capability we need and know we will attain. One of the best ways to become receptive to any force, particularly the forces of sound and vision, is to prepare for meditation properly. To implement our perception, we have to cleanse ourselves with light as we expand it around us in meditation. The more brightly and broadly we generate this light, the more clarity we will have. We will break up the discordant factors in our environment by the higher vibrations.

In everyday life, this process can be aided by color and sound. Music is effective because each tone influences the body in a different way according to its vibratory rate. Living with music and listening to it constantly can be elevating. But if you choose the wrong music for a particular effect, it can also break you down. The same is true of light and color. For instance, if you wear the wrong color or decorate your home in the wrong color, you will get undesirable results. If you take an emotionally high-strung youngster and put him in a red chair on a red rug in a room with red wallpaper, he will be ready to be locked up after half an hour. He would already have so much energy that red would put his energy beyond his level of control. On the other hand, if you were to put him in a nice cool, blue room, he would calm down. Do you think it is just an accident that surgical rooms have all been changed from white to aqua or turquoise? Have you ever thought about what color means? White of purity is mixed with green of growth and blue of healing to form turquoise. What better color for a hospital.

All these facts tell us that it is very important to become conscious of the colors and sounds surrounding us and of the effects they have on our daily lives. Once we understand these forces, we can use their power to bring a greater balance of experience into our existence.

How can light and sound be applied to our daily lives? What are they, really? How do they affect us? Where do they come from? Where do they go when they die away? A professor was once lecturing about light and illustrated his lecture with a candle. After the lecture, he blew the flame out. Some of the students asked where the light went. The teacher stood there, not knowing what to answer. Where do you think it went?

Prepare yourself as for creative meditation, and consider the essence of all sound — indeed, of all being — which is the om. The om, the Upanishads say, is the best and highest of all essences. It contains the highest vibration of all sounds; it is the sound of all sounds because it is all sound combined. This process of combination occurs by the means of cumulative transformation. As the latent forces and qualities of earth and water are concentrated, they vibrate higher. These vibrations create a more highly organized manifestation of spirit, which we call plant life. The plant forces, too, become concentrated and transmute into animal life, which is characterized by the demonstration of mental faculties. The highest vibration of animal life is the human being. We distinguish ourselves from all lower forms of life by the expression of our mental faculties in two forms of speech: the inner or conceptual and the outer or audible. Together these forms find their greatest harmony and fullest expression in the cosmic sound om.

As well as being the synthesis of all sounds, all essences, om is also the synthesis of all the manifestations of spirit. It is the apex of sound itself, ascended from the material plane to ultimate spiritualization and unification. Here it contains the latent properties of all the previous stages, just like a seed. It is not so strange that Buddhists call the om the *seed syllable,* for it holds latent all the potentialities of the earliest stages. And the earliest is light. We think that the creative source is light. Yes, but it is truth, too, and it is mercy. These are all aspects of universal being because its totality is not light. If it were all light, then light did not need to be created, did it? So God, or the universal, is a dazzling darkness. It absorbs all, it contains all, including you, whether you like it or not. At the same time, it reflects all truth, depending only on how it vibrates. God is the all and the nothingness, the ultimate essence that we sound in om.

This is hard for us to understand. For we are universal being. How we can be all and still be nothing? We understand it when we empty ourselves. In order to reach this state, we must lose the meaning of "I" and "mine" and work only with the "thou" within. Om is like a mirror reflecting all forms, all colors, and all sounds without changing its own nature. If we try to analyze the om, forming only an intellectual concept of it, we will never experience the nonrational and intangible quality of its essence.

Through the ages, om has become the essential means in the

practice of meditation because it is a shortening of the word *aum*. The meaning of the word *aum* is that the *a* stands for the subjective consciousness of the external world; the *u* stands for the consciousness of the inner world, the world of thoughts, feelings, desires, aspirations, and spiritual consciousness; and the *m* stands for the consciousness of the undifferentiated unity where there is no longer a split between the subjective and the objective. In Buddhism, this is called "the state of unqualified emptiness." This is the dazzling darkness, the void, the pulsating, velvety all and nothingness that is the greatest experience we can approach in our meditation. When we reach this, we know that visions are no longer necessary and that we have at this moment reached a oneness, an integration, with the universe. I have to admit it does not happen to me every day. But when it comes, I am very grateful, for then I indeed feel one with all that exists.

The subtle vibrations of sound play a very important role in mental association. The power of sound is greatly intensified as it crystallizes around individual experiences. The secret of this hidden power of sound or vibration forms the keys to the mysteries of creation. It can reveal the nature of things and of phenomenal life. Sounds can be used to integrate and disintegrate. Just to give you a hint about the power of sound, Caruso could shatter crystal and windowpanes with his high C, which had a pitch of 523.1 cycles per second. Imagine what a pitch of 759 cycles per second would do. That is the level achieved by some Tibetan monks in their chanting; they could literally bring down the roof. I want you to know the importance of sound. When I start chanting in front of my groups, some feel pain in their bodies from it, but it does not continue to hurt once the body gets broken down into a flowing substance again. In the beginning, I would advise you, don't chant aloud; do it mentally.

For millennia, om has been used to heighten vibrations. In the word *om* lies the totality of the universe, of all sounds. We are still very ignorant about these things. So it is better to hum the oms within yourself than to voice the oms aloud unless you know the harmonious tones of om.

The three different periods or episodes in the time of silence are related to the three aspects of being. These aspects are the physical, where the sacrum and the spleen are principally involved; the emotional, where the solar plexis is principally involved; and the atonement, where the heart is principally involved. The plane of at-one-ment is the seat of consciousness, the plane of harmony, of union, the place where we bring the physical forces together with the spiritual forces. When we do this, we become mentally conscious of this harmony; we start expressing it in our daily lives. We are in balance, and the heart has become the fulcrum of our being. Understand that we speak constantly of the heart of love. This is not the physical heart. It is that focus of the plane of consciousness that draws the physical forces toward itself and fuses them with the light forces from the spiritual plane. This union finds its worldly expression in spiritual action.

The oms are chanted in three different levels. The first om is a soft chant. The effect of the soft chant is to contract the head centers, causing higher vibrations that will still the lower vibrations of the conscious mind. Because it is so high, this vibration from the head centers will drive out coarse particles and create finer ones. Then we have etheric, monadic particles. The vibrations will flow from your head centers to your heart and from your heart to the base of your spine. They move through the body in the form of a vortex, activating the pineal, the pituitary, the thyroid gland (the high centers). These centers radiate their energy out toward the thymus.

The second om is medium loud and stabilizes the emotional plane, the solar plexus. It contacts and sets in motion the heart center, for that heart has to start pumping to draw up the physical forces from the lower planes to merge them with the light forces from the spiritual plane, collected now in the thymus. Thus, the heart again becomes the fulcrum, the plane of atonement, union, or harmony. It drives out coarse matter and stills the emotional or feeling body, making it the true reflector of the divine self. The vibrations go only toward the heart.

The third om is loud for physical reasons. The effects are similar to those of the second om but primarily concern the double or etheric body. What is the double or etheric body? Surrounding the physical body is an etheric body that is exactly the form and shape of the human body, enclosing it completely. It is nothing other than all the vibrations of the total being. We could also call this the auric body, for this is what we see when we see the aura. The aura is the vibration of the etheric body. It could also be called the astral body or the feeling body.

The feeling body is connected by a toll bridge to the physical body. During the night, when our etheric or astral or feeling body needs to expand itself into the universe to gather universal forces, the physical body remains quiet, to gain physical strength from the plane on which it exists. The etheric body closes off the toll bridge. No one can go in or out. When you sleep, you do not feel pain because your feeling body is closed off. Under an anesthetic, your etheric bridge has actually been closed off. Under hypnosis, we can have the suggestion that we close off the etheric bridge. Someone once asked if I prepared myself before I went on the bed of nails and the answer was no. I only close off my etheric bridge. Then I feel no pain. But in addition, I remain conscious yet unattached to my body. In this state of nonattachment, my physical body suffers none of the trauma or distress that would usually accompany puncture wounds. I have not just repressed a pain so that my consciousness is unaware of it; there is no pain to feel.

I have said that the primary effects of the third om are on the etheric body. Very high vibrating people are very sensistive people, for they pick up pains and feelings at the edges of their expanding etheric bodies. A very sensitive person is often vibrating at a very high rate because he or she is a spiritual being and has more psychic ability. That doesn't mean that every psychic (or those who call themselves psychics) is spiritual, too, but merely that this ability is a part of everyone's spiritual growth. The third om creates a shell of vibrations around the individual as a protective shield. This is both a shield of light and a shield of sound.

Again, I would caution you not to chant the om aloud at home because you might not get the right intonations. Remember, you are using a power so strong that an irregular tone can upset you and the world around you. Just do it within yourself.

The order of the om chanting is as follows: the first om is chanted three times; then, a period of silence is maintained. Next, the second om is chanted three times and is followed by another period of silence. Finally, the third om is chanted three times, then a period of silence. That makes nine chantings in all. Each om is chanted three times in order to divide the meditation into three different levels: the envisaging, the subjective, and the abstract.

After the first oms, the first time of silence will create all kinds of colors, usually in little geometric figures such as triangles, stars, flashes of light. After the second oms, the vibrations will cause particles within you to break up, becoming streaks of colors and then becoming objects, scenes, symbols, or feelings. All kinds of experiences can happen on all levels of the inner senses. You might smell certain scents. You might feel a tremor go through your body. These are all symptoms of the new inner sense, awakened by the energy flowing to you. After the third oms, I suggest focusing on an abstract idea, perhaps a theme from a reverie. You can use an abstract word such as *love* and create this vibration love. See what you can feel for yourselves. This can bring you to high vibrations where you are capable of drawing from the universe new energies, new substances.

Chant other sounds in order to resonate with various specific aspects of the cosmos. Meditation with mantras using different sounds from the om bring in a different flow of the forces that also stimulate the finer subtle forces, the finer particles within you. Mantras create a flow that is like the resonance, the reverberation of sounds occurring within a field of two or more tuning forks. The tones of a tuning fork will sound when you hit it; the second fork will pick it up and resound by resonance, by reverberation. Therefore, every tone you utter in your mantras will tune in, reverberate, attract to you and absorb by resonance all the tones of the same kind from everywhere in the universe. This is what mantra meditation is designed to do: to help you tune in to some aspect of the cosmos. You should chant your mantras before your silent period, not during the silent period. Begin by thinking about the words in the mantra during the preparatory breathing exercise for about eight counts in the beginning. Many people become confused with just counting, for they spend more time counting to themselves than tending to their breathing. But these technicalities are of little concern once you have adapted your meditation to your own rhythms. For now, it is simply important to note the purpose of saying these mantras.

In the silence of meditation, we can hear the cosmic sounds. There are ten sounds that we can recognize in meditation. Often people hear only the third sound; the first two sounds are very hard to hear.

The first sound is not the sound of an instrument; it is a sound like *chin*. The second sound is a double *chin, chin*. The third sound, which many people have heard in meditation, is like ringing clocks or bells. The next sound is like that of a conch, a seashell. The fifth sound is a lute. The sixth is cymbals. The seventh is the flute. The eighth is a drum. The ninth is a double drum. Finally, you will hear a roaring sound like thunder, and suddenly it dies out.

The reason that few people hear all ten is that we are able to pick out of the universe only certain vibrations that are audible to us physically as well as to our inner senses. Vibrations at the extreme low and high ranges are beyond our normal capacity.

This is what is called the music of the spheres, of which Pythagoras taught. We can absorb these sounds through attracting them out of the universe; we should be able to create or recreate these sounds and manifest them. This is the case not only with music but with all the universal qualities. We can attract and use them in creative expression, if not for ourselves, then to inspire others to seek a similar at-one-ment.

USE THE OM
TO CLEAR YOUR CENTERS

The average person using the om chant correctly will experience the sound of om flowing through all the centers. We use the om chant also to clear out the centers. It becomes like a pipe cleaner, for when all these forces under pressure go through them, the centers are cleaned out.

Many people like to meditate upon the forehead because they have heard this is the godhead or Christ center. They concentrate very hard on just that center and do not think about any other center. But if the forces have to go throughout the whole body, what good does it do if I open only this center? People who become spiritual fanatics often become mentally unstable because of the concentration of light in one place. It is never distributed throughout the body, so its pressure becomes so intense that eventually it blows their top. This is what is meant by blowing your top, getting so much pressure from the inside that it really blows all the fuses in your brain. In the beginning, if you are not sure that all your senses are opened, you'd better not meditate on only one center. It is safest to meditate on different centers; perhaps beginning with your heart center, for that is where you become conscious of all the forces. Or meditate on your throat center, which will reflect that light down to the lower planes. Your thyroid gland is the mirror to reflect radiance when vibrations are shifting from the physical plane to the mental plane. I did not say, "Do not meditate on the forehead." You can meditate on the forehead once you are sure all the centers are open. But *do not* meditate on your solar plexus. This is your emotional plane, and you would concentrate so much energy there that you would be completely incapable of meditation. It would stir up everything in your life. It is the seat of emotions, the center of activity that must become intuitive through spiritual growth.

There are spiritual disciplines that contemplate the solar plexus, and their devotees go into ecstasy because they become emotionally involved with their God. They cry, shout, moan, gesture, jump, and bat their heads against a wall. These are not the vibrations we are seeking. It is important for you to know what systems are involved, what the centers are, and what regions of your body are influenced by your meditation. Then, you can learn to detect an imbalance in the thorax, in the chest, or in your heart center and correct it.

Heart diseases are caused because of lack of consciousness of an imbalance. Why do we get ulcers? Because of a surplus of energy in the solar plexus that starts churning the low negative vibrations. People in business experience this. They do not have a way of releasing their pressures; they have an inflow through the pituitary but no outflow.

The spleen is one of the most beautiful instruments in our bodies; it is your extra battery. Energies go from one center to another. From the base of the spine, they go directly to the pituitary; from the solar plexus, straight to the heart. But the only ones that go to all the centers emanate from the spleen. When athletes running a race become exhausted, they feel a pain in the spleen for a couple of seconds and then feel recharged to run as fast as ever. Why? The pain is nothing more than an indication that their regular energy has run out. When the spleen is activated, it hurts. When the athlete starts feeling stronger again, the spleen is giving energy to all the other centers. This is the purpose of the spleen.

There are also effects on the spine that can be regulated in meditation. When the centers become clogged, it causes a blockage in a particular vertebra. How many people can hardly sit on a chair because their tailbone begins to hurt? How many people go about with a lower backache in the lumbar region? It is due to a concentration of forces in this region. Many older people who get no exercise mentally or physically become obstructed in the abdomen, which causes constipation. The finer particles become very solid through the action of lower vibrations; they cannot bring themselves up to higher vibrations or throw off the energy that they would normally be able to draw in. Therefore, there is a solidification in the abdominal area, accompanied by lower backache.

How many of us who reach a rather high spiritual level in our daily lives eventually have thyroid trouble? This is because we do not reflect the light from above to our lower centers. We develop a defective thyroid by starving it of the energy it requires.

The pituitary is the door through the medulla oblongata for the manifestation of psychic phenomena. It has more than that to do, however, because in the sacral area are the gonads and the hormone centers. Is it then so strange that some yogis become celibates? They want to use the hormones to feed the pituitary, thereby breaking more quickly the cycle of rebirth. By not using their hormones to create children, they create one child only, the bodhisattva or Christ Child within their own self. Some yogis even specialize in certain exercises to encourage these hormones to go from the gonads to the pituitary, though they are already in direct contact.

The highest center is the pineal body. Medical research knows very little about it. From a spiritual viewpoint, however, we know that this is the door through which the total light enters. All these centers are influenced by all sounds and therefore by om because om is the totality of all sounds.

Conclude your meditation by gently reawakening to the outside world. After a last period of silence, you have to bring yourself back to waking consciousness, to bring yourself into conscious control again. Otherwise, at the end of a meditation, you may be left in a state of confusion. Yoga teaches that real expansion is to have your head in the clouds with both feet steady on the floor. A person may have a marvelous high, but nothing results from being that high. It has to become practical, otherwise it has no meaning. How do we do that? By chanting the same loud om (three times) but in a lower tone. To enter the silence you used a different sound, a higher and softer sound.

After humming (inside yourself) the three oms, stay passive. You need to create a body consciousness again. Feel the weight of your body, realize the environment you are in, but don't move your body yet. Just become aware of every part of your body: your circulation, your heartbeat, your senses. Slightly squint your eyes; and then, open your eyes very slowly. Never jump out of meditation. Before you move, very slowly come back until your eyes get used to the light again.

I know that many people won't want to come back when they're in that state of deep silence. Many people may lose track of this (or any) method along the way, as perhaps you will. Don't be upset with yourself, please. If you go on your own way, that is marvelous. Any method is there to guide you. If you want to go off on your own and you know your way, never let method stop you in meditation because you then disrupt your own pattern. In the beginning, you may get some physiological responses such as pressure on the forehead or on top of the head, choking, a little reverberation, a tremor through the body. There are reasons for this. You are putting your body into action with new energy, intensifying the energy that you already have. Do not allow such reactions to frighten or disturb you. Keep your aim high and clear, and continue on the way.

SIX

THE BURNING
AND THE LOVING

Now that we know something about meditation, I want to talk
about the paths we follow when we begin to apply the insight
and the power we obtain through meditation to our lives here
on earth. One is the path of love, which is the one I am going to
talk about in this chapter. Another is the path of action, which
we will come to in Chapter 7.

THE INNER FIRE

There is a kindling flame, a power for inspiration, eternal,
pure, and subtle, that permeates our intuitive powers and can
kindle the expressions of this intuition. It is the inner fire. This
inner fire is the totality of the light forces that we, as humankind, can draw in and have flow through us. They are the
forces that prod us into a spiritual action through awareness.
But they can only prod us into action if we attain a higher
frequency of vibration. We must raise our vibrations high
enough so that they become equal to the most subtle force (the
etheric), wherein lies all the wisdom of the ages. Then, au-

tomatically by resonation, we will draw in energy from the universal paraconscious mind. This can kindle the flame of inspiration.

The inner fire, the creative principle, affects matter as well as mind because it acts upon the paraconscious mind. It heals by breaking down coarse, solid matter in the body. You cannot be without this inner fire. You are existing because of it. Even after you die, the inner fire remains with your body to fuel the process of decay. The body is finally disintegrated by the cosmic inner fire that transmutes material mass back into its original state — from dust to dust. And new bodies will be formed from that released energy. Remember, there is nothing new in the universe. Substance is always used again. It cannot disappear. Where can it go? Temporarily, it may be invisible, but it never disappears. Perhaps it will reappear in a different form or shape, but it is always there as prime substance, spirit. Therefore, all matter can be called spirit. But all spirit cannot be called matter because what has not materialized is still spirit; for example, what we call etheric light has not yet been formally manifested.

In our minds or consciousnesses, inner fire is the forming, order-creating principle through which understanding and truth are born. How does it do this? When this fire becomes active in matter, it transmutes it, diffuses it into less dense forms. It has the same effect upon nonmaterial processes; the blockages disappear, and truth gets a chance to rise in your awareness. Truth is pure spirit. It is always with you, and you are free when you can finally feel it flowing. That release is the influence of the inner fire upon both mind and matter.

In the spiritual realm, the inner fire lifts us beyond our physical beings. The flame within you can rise so high that you no longer are aware of your physical body; you merge with all the forces surrounding you. Complete disintegration and integration take place. Integration and disintegration are brother and sister; they always come together. Whenever you want to integrate into something, you will have to disintegrate something else. If you create something, you change something else. If you cut a tree, it does not cease to exist, even if you make a table out of it; but you have changed that tree. Every creative process is like that. Life and death are examples of the same cycle. You must disintegrate physically before you integrate with the light forces. Then, when you want to become physical again, you disintegrate from the light forces and you integrate with the physical forces. And the effects of these changes are cumulative. Each transformation is an experience from which we learn. By learning, we perceive more and more until finally we no longer alternate. Finally, the soul has perceived so much of the nature of the cosmos that it merges with the universal paraconscious mind. It has become aware that it *is* the mind and has no need for a physical body any longer.

The inner fire thus lifts us beyond the narrow boundaries of our individuality and above this self-created world of ours. It *is* a self-created world, my friends, not a world that was created by someone else. You created this physical world by inner fire. You created this physical body by inner fire. You had to individualize yourself because you had to learn to become aware and then return, upward. You create; you destroy. We are very good at destroying; in creating, we are running behind. But one of these days, we will realize the meaning of balance.

The flame also dissolves and transforms all that was frozen and rigid. When the mind and body become rigid, resulting in painful conditions such as arthritis, they can become flexible again when we learn to release and express our inner flame.

Just as worlds are born from the power of the flame, so they are dissolved by the same force. Inner fire is as creative as it is liberating, in the sense that inner fire is the source of both human desire and the desire for truth. To speak more plainly, it is the feeling that in its lowest forms is like a blazing straw fire nourished by momentary enthusiasms and emotional urges. In its highest form, it is the flame of inspiration, nourished by spiritual insight. Both forms have the nature of fire, but the straw fire burns out quickly, starved for fuel.

We should not underestimate the force of emotion, for it is very powerful. When you allow this force to amplify your individual desires, it can lead, for instance, to a misuse of your sex life and of your ambitions. But if it is aimed toward the heart, it will converge with the light of the cosmos. Together, they create spiritual desire, which is like a laser beam, capable of disintegrating any obstacle or negativity. Only with this desire can you disintegrate animosity, for the hate people express makes steel appear soft. Hate is a tremendous force, completely destructive. Love is a tremendous force, too, but it can undo hate only if there is a complete purification of all that is in you. Even a little resentment within us adds to the power of hate, so we have an inner duty to perform. We must release ourselves from hate and resentment. We have to transmute the forces chained there so that they become part of our loving power.

Once we become aware of the forces within us and realize the presence of this light, we must immediately use it in proper ways. I cannot overemphasize the importance of this crucial point. Let it become practical. You can read inspirational literature that is much more elegant than my words, but if you cannot make it practical, then you are not understanding it. We are practical beings. We must learn to operate beyond the waking state, to become fully aware, and then know how to handle our potential here in the practical world. This aim should be the focus of all our acts and thoughts.

We should recognize that the warmth of emotion is part of inspiration, a state in which we truly and completely forget ourselves in the experience of the higher reality. The act of self-surrender frees and transforms our innermost beings. It is what we call the spiritual ecstasy, absorption, spiritual vision. The coldness of conceptual understanding is opposed by the heat of emotion, seized by the irresistible force of truth. Truth is never cold; it is never sharp, either. It is harmonious, melodious, rhythmic, peaceful, warm, tender, and gentle. Oh, sometimes we say the truth is harsh. But it is we who make the truth harsh because our tongues are so very sharp. Sometimes, we can speak truth and still be gentle with it, too, if we put the loving aspects of our powers behind it. Intellectual comprehension establishes a subject-object relationship in which the comprehending subject remains on the outside, separated from the object, and it is cold. Emotion, however, is a dynamic attitude, a moving toward, or a merging with, the object of contemplation, an effort to catch up with its movement until we are one with it and are able to experience it from within, in its intrinsic nature, in its particular rhythm, thereby attaining the awareness of harmony with it.

For example, when you approach a person or a problem, don't become emotional or suddenly enthusiastic. Contemplate this person or problem until it seems to be part of you. Merge into that being until you feel that you are one with this being; then act upon this oneness.

We often fail to see and fail to hear because we so abruptly and coldly form concepts and judgments. To be moved is an act of spiritual participation. To become one with the subject of our contemplation, we must synthesize our own spiritual, mental, emotional, and physical aspects. When this inner unification has been attained, we are capable of clear and balanced perceptions. Our bodies will also express this balance and will be healthier.

The warmth of emotion can be transmuted into the flame of inspiration. To me, inspiration is revelation, in the sense that suddenly, with incredible certainty and subtlety, something becomes visible and audible, shaking us and overpowering us to our deepest beings. Our bodies are filled with bliss down to the tips of our toes. We listen, we do not search or ask who is giving. Like lightning, a thought flashes up with necessity, without hesitation, without regard to its form. We have no choice; inspiration is a state of our being completely beside ourselves, a depth of happiness in which all that is painful and dark acts, not as a contradiction, but as a necessary condition. It is involuntary, and that is the most remarkable aspect of inspiration. We haven't the slightest idea what the root image is or what the stimulus is. Everything offers itself as the nearest, the most adequate, the simplest expression. The light of the inspiration fills us completely, so that it finally emanates beyond us. A vortex surrounds us, embracing us completely, and we dwell in a state of wisdom and knowing.

The universe is progressing through our inspiration, and when the universe embraces us, we can embrace it. That's the beauty of it. Inspiration has a dual nature; one is the cosmic, and the other is the individual. There is no true difference between the cosmos and the individual, although the one seems separate from the other. Inner fire bridges this separation through the incorporation and integration of all qualities.

The bridge of inner fire is in the heart. That is where the increasing illumination of the mind and the gradual transfiguration of the body have their source. These changes are a matter of degree and are manifested by the control and order that mind and body impose on one another. Spirit controls them both. How the body grows is an expression of your spirit. The mind is a battery filled with energy and spirit; but unless something is connected to this battery, no expression can take place.

To manifest the spirit means to guide your personal awareness by the perception of the universal order and then to form a connection between mind (the battery) and the body (its physical instrument). An active spirituality harnesses soul, mind, and body to work as one. Spirituality is acting as a total being. Therefore, if you are not active on all three planes of being, any nourishment you absorb will become coarse, solidified, and crystallized and, like cholesterol in the arteries, will make your physical, spiritual, and mental arteries narrower and narrower. A person who has arteriosclerosis has a hard time walking because the blood can hardly get to the feet; eventually such a person might become completely crippled.

You can become crippled spiritually if you do not *act* spiritually. Even polishing your shoes can be a spiritual act because anything you do should have your heart in it.

"Put your heart into it" means to project your cosmic light from the heart into the physical power to act. The candle does not have a flame without being lighted. When I light a candle, I may imagine it has all its strength right in the wax. But it needs power from the atmosphere. If I cover the top, the flame dies. When this power stops flowing, the wax gets hard again. As soon as there is fire, the wax starts melting, even dripping away. The flame grows as it consumes more wax, and the wax becomes more subtle the higher the flame glows because it frees the higher forces that are within it.

INTEGRATE THE PHYSICAL
AND MENTAL INTO THE SPIRITUAL

It makes no sense to read glowing phrases that tell me about God and Nirvana or even that the sky is blue. If I am blind, I cannot experience them. They didn't tell me how to open my eyes, so what is it to me that the sky is blue? That is what is lacking in spiritual teachings that are only spoken, not practiced. When I speak to people about raising their vibrations, one of the first questions I'm asked is, "How?" You really want to know; you are still very innocent, like a child who simply wants practical answers. I think that attitude is a good one because we need to develop spiritual muscle. And you must not only develop spiritual muscles; you must keep also them active, flex them, expand them constantly. Your goal is not the making of muscles but the building of a coordinated instrument that can work for you if you keep it active.

You may have heard some teachers speak about being rid of this body of ours. Let us understand this in a practical way. While in meditation, we may lose consciousness of the body. But it is essential to realize that this letting go of the body brings it into better condition and allows healing to take place. You have to go to higher sources to find healing for the body. Healing is not just a physical matter; it is also a spiritual matter. We have to include it in the process of spiritual development because the body is, after all, the temple we temporarily live in. To bring a spiritual healing to your body and soul, your state must be one in which the duality of the body and soul no longer exists. Integration is the goal. Remember, we disintegrate the physical by integration with the spiritual. By disintegration, of course, we mean that the imperfect, disharmonious physical expressions are broken down. Then they are brought together again in the physical equivalent of divine order. This is integration of mind and body through the manifestation of the spiritual.

Among bodily, mental, and spiritual functions, there is only a difference in degree, not in essence, because all that exists is spirit. We experience this in our physical forms as a continuum of vibrations, with spirit at one end and matter at the other.

When the mind has become luminous, the body must partake of this luminous nature. This is the reason for the radiation that we see emanating from enlightened beings, portrayed by artists as the halo and aura surrounding saints and deities. The force field that surrounds each of us became so luminous around them that it was visible to the physical eye. Most of us are blind to this radiation, but it can be seen by those who have developed their spiritual eyes as a direct effect of inner fire.

When this emanation is at a high frequency, all its colors merge together, so that it is not a multicolored aura anymore but a single hue. In this flame of devotion and self-surrender, the light of love and the warmth of the heart are united. This is equivalent to the correspondence existing between the forces of day and of night. The perfect person combines both sides of reality, the depth of the night and the light of the day, the darkness of the all-embracing space and the light of the suns and the stars.

Do you realize that you can see the light of the stars and the suns only because of the darkness of the sky? But they both have to be there. It is the all-embracing darkness that reflects the light. Because it is the darkness that lets you become aware of light, you cannot separate the two. The creative, primordial power of life and the luminous power of wisdom are the two sides of one organic whole. If they are developed separately, they remain barren and incapable of unfolding their natures and their meanings. So don't just enlarge your spiritual muscle; tone that muscle by exercising it in the way you live.

HOW CAN WE USE THE INNER FIRE TO BENEFIT OURSELVES AND OTHERS?

Bless anything you give, anything you take, no matter how dark it is. Darkness is the necessary predecessor of the light, just as negativeness is the necessary predecessor for the absorption of the positive. That is why you should love your enemies; there is love in their animosity, and it is up to you to find it. If you can see the beauty in an adversary, hidden in that dark cave, you know that in that dark cave there is the spark of light that you can unite with your own spark to become a flame of love. Then give your adversary the vibrancy of your own love. If your gift is accepted, your enemy's own flame will burn brighter.

How do you fan another's dim spark? Surround others with your own light; express your love for them. How do you go about putting this light around yourself? I don't insist on a visualization because that word *visualization* tends to emphasize the least important aspect of spiritual experience. Many people will not be able to see or visualize light. Nevertheless, they must realize that they are light themselves.

When you want to put light around you (as I explained on page 70), you will seem to be looking deep into the back of your brain and down a spiraled tube, at the end of which you will see a tiny spot of light. That is the pilot light, the serpent fire of kundalini. When you have mentally moved into this spiral, flashes of light suddenly start coming from your toes up through your body, and all your cells are permeated with this light. You feel more vibrant, and a small tremor might go through you as you fill yourself with light. The light should be expelled from the forehead, and it will form a vortex around you. The higher you vibrate, the higher and wider the flame grows.

An act of love, the deep sincerity of loving a being no matter what that being is, also creates this acceleration of light. When the expanded field of vibrations is formed, it insulates you from all negative forces that are at a lower level. If your energy field is of a certain electric potency, then nothing below that electric potency can penetrate it. Higher forces can enter, but anything below will disintegrate.

This entails an unlearning process. The subconscious mind has to be retrained out of all the doctrines and attitudes that have been filling it; they must be transmuted. The subconscious is a most beautiful, subtle, flexible instrument, especially in its ability to act as a tape recorder with an automatic replay. As soon as a certain familiar action begins, the subconscious mind automatically switches on a response. The unlearning process therefore is a most important task. To teach new things to the unconscious is easy because it has been teaching itself all your life without your awareness. To become consciously aware of what we know is both essential and difficult. I must become consciously aware every day before I counsel because I have to protect myself from the negative vibrations uncovered during counseling. Not only do I have to protect myself, but I must be able to see these problems clearly. I will not be able to know them unless I myself am clear and subtle. I have to permeate those who come to me in order to become them and feel their needs. Discernment is clear seeing. We will have it only when we have become so subtle that we can permeate other beings, be one with them, and experience what they are experiencing.

The inner fire is a force flowing in and flowing out, a circulating force. But without your conscious involvement, there will be no proper circulation. Without proper circulation, your psychic centers clog up with grosser crystallizations. The narrower these centers become, the harder it is for the light to flow through. We have to keep the centers as wide open as possible, and they can only stay open when the vibrations go through with a tremendous speed, which, in turn, will disintegrate solid matter. The increase of vibrations, of inner fire, can be amplified by joining yourself with others. You join, not to get something from them, but to share. If you can do that, then you will not just feel your neighbor as your brother, for he will not be your brother anymore; he will be you. You have no brothers and sisters. You have only you because you are the totality. You are reflected within every other one, and they, in turn, are totality, too. To do this is to feel the merging of light, a tremendous love and ecstasy, not an emotional ecstasy on the human side of passion, but an ecstasy of exuberance, a vibratory state that you can hardly describe.

Of course, a prayer group or meditation group can achieve a tremendous healing capacity because they can become a blazing forest fire. There is not water enough in the whole world to extinguish such a spiritual fire. It runs on and merges and emanates rays of light. It penetrates every substance, even the densest solids, because they are only solid according to our conscious concept. They are never solid in reality. So this fire penetrates every particle. When inner fire becomes a blazing force, it becomes pure white light, the finest subtle substance we can reach in this lifetime. This is why the halo is symbolized by the white light, not by any other hue. "Only through me will you know thy father." Only through the white light will you be able to become universal being. Then you meet the source because after the white light, what happens? We go into the void; suddenly, we are surrounded by darkness. But what a darkness it is. The absorption of everything that exists, an embrace within which all things are united. When you enter this dark embrace, you are not *a* being; you *are* being. You are not *a* spirit; you *are* spirit. You are not *a* god; you *are* God. If you can just hold onto those moments and live them after they pass, then you will really live every step you take. Remember, you were, you are, and you always will be one with God. You are the cosmos. The Hindus say it beautifully, "I am that." "That" means everything.

SEEK YOUR OWN WAY
TO THE FLAME OF INNER FIRE

The search for inner fire may lead some of you into nature, to the forests or mountains. The old masters went to mountaintops to meditate because they thought they would be closer to God. Do you know where I found God? Hidden in my heart. Yes, that is true. But under what circumstances? During World War II, when some Nazis were whipping me. That was when I suddenly became aware of my oneness. I had been in the woods and mountains before, as a Boy Scout. It did not mean anything to me then; it was just beautiful. But I did not find God then. I found truth through suffering. I meet people who are natural people, nature people, who should go as much as possible into nature because they have a tremendous love and need for it. That is the only place where they might possibly find peace of mind. At the same time, there are other people who can be in the woods for a week and only yearn to go back to their friends. So don't fashion generalities. Let us become aware of our own paths and allow others to have their own. In the end, what is most important is that we act upon the fruits of our searches. We must demonstrate our beings as they are motivated by inner fire and guided by truth. If any holy man or any prophet had hidden his knowledge and had never given any demonstration of his being, we would never have learned about our own potentials.

In meditation, we encounter the inner fire, and a process of transmutation begins. This happens when we open ourselves and attract the light energy. When it comes in contact with our physical beings, it becomes fire. It is finally concentrated within our physical beings at the base of the spine, remaining there as fire until we raise it and use it as a force for transmutation. This force finally purifies us. And when purification takes place, all the grosser particles in our bodies become so fine and so subtle that the fire again becomes light. So it leaves us as it came in. It comes in in its full purity, and it should go out in its full purity. It is a cycle without a beginning, without an end, because even after you cease to exist in the physical plane, you are still working with the same fire on another level of being. You will adapt a different form or shape on other levels of consciousness but still exist out of the same substance. The only change is that each new level is more subtle until finally you are again the creative substance, spirit. You never cease to exist as spirit. You cease to exist in the forms and shapes that this spirit can manifest on that level of consciousness you have reached. This is why highly developed beings can disintegrate and integrate at will. They seemingly appear and disappear to our physical eyes. We see them disappear, but we know that they are still there, only in a more subtle substance. It is not a change of substance. The body is still there; but it has become so subtle that our limited vision cannot register the fine light rays emanating from it.

Usually you can see only what is gross. The room you are in is filled with billions of beings in their subtleness. Every vibration of your cells is heard and influenced by all the beings in the universe and will influence the vibration of other beings no matter what their manifestation is. Subconsciously, you are a walking sponge drawing things to you, attracting vibrations as subtle or as dense as those within your subconscious mind.

The problem of the whole of humanity is that we are only aware of what is grossly visible, touchable, tasteable, smellable, and so on. This is why we have to go into meditation; through meditation, we become aware of what we are not normally cognizant. The inner fire we find there is what arouses us from the slumber of worldly contentment and tears us away from the routine of mundane life. But after meditation, we go back among our fellow creatures, and this is where the burning power of love comes in. First, we go through the action of putting a light force around us, to be separated from whatever can disturb us in a negative way. When we have begun the path toward enlightenment, we use this same light force to embrace our fellow creatures and become one with them. We spread the warmth of spiritual emotion.

There is very little that can ever approach and break this sheath of love unless you do it yourself. A person who gets it loves all and hates none. This person will be satisfied and content forever. There is nothing this earth can offer that measures up to this love because this person will have set foot on a path that leads to the unmanifested God, the unobstructed universe, the completion of the universal consciousness.

This path of love is greater than any of the others, greater than the path of action or the path of knowledge or the path of wisdom, for the path of love is the one that must be followed first. Of course, we have to realize that many of these pathways have little side roads. We do not always stay on the same path. It is not up to us to judge anyone who chooses to take the straight way or a winding road uphill or the road through the valleys, down first and then up, or a crooked road with very sharp edges. We may wish to have some companionship on our own path. We should acknowledge this and should never judge anyone by saying, "You are not on the right path." The only judgment anyone can truly make is, "Am I on the right path myself?"

If you think that your path is better, prove that it is better by *being* better, not by *talking* better. Be an example of your pathway. Then other people will automatically be attracted by the energy you emanate, and they may choose to follow your path. But don't try to persuade anyone to follow a particular pathway. If someone asks you for a road map, then you should answer. But you should refrain from saying which path is the better one for that person. You can say that a particular path presents this and that obstacle, but leave it at that. Remember that no matter what path someone chooses, all go to the same place: the place of illumination and all-consciousness.

As for you, you will have begun to know of truth; you will have begun to become aware of, and awake to, what you are. You will not feel separated anymore, distant from others or from the divine inner knowledge called God. How could you feel separate from a truth that we live in every thought and action? For you, it will no longer be a case of the divine being somewhere in the clouds and you being down here in this sad world. You will know the divine within yourself. By expressing your heart, you will be expressing God. You will feel illuminated, annointed, and inspired to share this awareness with others. You will indeed know peace, inwardly and outwardly. You can confidently pursue your ultimate aim: to reach the apex, to know yourself, to be self-realized.

If your confidence falters, reconfirm it by meditating on the perfection within you. Each of us can doubt. Each of us is like an earthen vessel that says, "I wonder if I can be filled with water? I wonder if I am breakable, if I can be put in the oven to be fired?" But these are really silly questions for an earthen vessel to ask because it should know the qualities of the clay from which it was made. If we want to achieve self-realization, then we must ask ourselves, "What is our substance?" When we know the answer, then all the qualities of our substance will be our qualities. All God's qualities will be our qualities because the potter who made us is the universal mind, and the clay is spirit substance.

Because we were created out of pure spirit, we, too, are capable of creation. We are cocreators because we are individualized aspects of this universal being. Through our individualized paraconscious minds, we partake of the universal order. We are perfect, but we are behind closed doors and often asleep. If this spirit substance is always perfect, so are we. Our spirit substance is always perfect although our individualized minds do not always bring out this perfection and therefore our bodies do not bring our perfection into expression either. We must become aware of our qualities and start bringing them forth in a physical expression and a physical creativity. For when we create, we add strength to ourselves and strength to the universe. This keeps the universe in motion. If we stop being creators, we stop life. Life is constant creativity, constant change, constant motion.

Meditation is the concentration of our attention away from the ephemeral, changing world outside us. It is the focusing upon our internal realities so that we can open the doors to our inner chambers and awaken the perfect self within. Remember, meditation does not create the perfection. It makes us aware that we are, in essence, perfect. Our spirits are in the image of God, and they share the divine attributes. Our physical forms are just episodes of our spiritual existences. Our minds, as part of the universal mind, helped create this earth, this physical plane, and we will create many more planets after this one.

It is hard to comprehend that we are such small beings and at the same time the totality of all beings. But only by understanding this will we realize what our function is in this universe and strive for its fulfillment. Meditation helps us to realize this and lets us replenish our inner fire according to our needs.

Other methods can help, but be careful. Reading spiritually insightful or beautiful literature can be very rewarding. But be sure to put the heat of your love into this experience. In my youth, my family would read the Bible together. I would get sick after each reading because I didn't understand a word of it. There was no love in the proceeding. It was never done with feeling, with understanding, or with expression. It was a rigid, barren, spiritual ritual. If it had been a creative spiritual ritual, I could have accepted it, but it was not.

Love is the easiest path to follow and the heart of all other paths. Love is the most natural way. It does not involve analytic or abstract discussion of the cosmos or of God, but rather avoids it. The followers of this path of love and devotion have a faith based on as simple and pure a love as that of a child for its parents. That feeling is the warmth that enlivens our hearts and nourishes our spirit.

Our society does not encourage us to love. We are encouraged to become analytic and rational. Perhaps these attitudes give us greater control, but they also suppress our emotional and sentimental experiences. I have met people who claim that they have beautiful control, but their stomachs are ulcerated by that "control." They are able to restrain themselves from expressing what is in their hearts and only speak what their rational judgments have approved. They hold the intensity of emotion within themselves, and it soon begins to devour them, ulcerating their bodies and producing anxiety in their minds. We must learn that suppression and repression are not the only means by which we can gain control. Through love and understanding, we can attain a far greater control because it will be based on empathy rather than on fear.

Have you ever seen eyes change from sadness into beauty? Once when I was giving a lecture, the whole auditorium was dark, and I was standing in the spotlight. I could not see the audience at all. But right in front of me were two black eyes, two beautiful black eyes, dripping with sadness. Wherever I looked, these eyes followed me. Whatever I felt, these eyes were directed at me. They were begging for recognition. When the lecture was over, people lined up to say hello, to shake hands, to ask personal questions. Inwardly, I was still hurting because of those eyes. Suddenly I found myself confronted with them. On an impulse, I threw my arms around that person and kissed her. The eyes belonged to a black girl who had been rejected by everybody in society, by her father, by her mother, by her brothers and sisters. She was torn apart and crying inwardly. I heard a sigh go through the audience, a sigh of disgust. "How dare he shock us this way! How dare he, while his wife stands next to him, express his love. Does he know that he is part of this society?" Yes, I am. But if that means that I cannot express love, I would rather not belong to it.

A path is one vision of how to move toward our universal

aim. It can be a guide and focus and help us. But all paths also have dangers along the way. These require that we develop spiritual strength and discernment. The disadvantage of the path of love is that it can become a terrible fanaticism. Many followers of Eastern and Western religious movements were, and still are, elitist and fanatic in their belief that their way is the only right way. To be solely attached to an object of love is a very beautiful virtue. But we must remember that claiming God to be omnipresent means to love and to be attached to all that was created in this universe, not just one path or one aspect or one teaching.

It is not just our own level of being that we should love; we should also love the levels beneath us: the flowers, the trees, the insects, the animals, the birds, the rocks, the sands, the mountains, the seas, and the oceans. They are all part of you, and you are part of them. How can we be so blind, not to see, not to feel that all this is in us? Have we forgotten that all the minerals found in this planet are within our physical substances? How can we deny our connection to them? Have we forgotten that all the vegetable substances on earth are within our chemical structures? How can we deny that we are part of all the vegetables and plants and trees and flowers? Have we forgotten that our bodies are completed by animal substances? That is what the human being is: minerals, vegetables, and animals. How can you deny your attachment to all creatures? How can you despise any of God's creatures? Attachment to a single object has let the undeveloped mind present one ideal of God as the *only* possible concept of God, thereby hating and despising any other concept or ideal of God. Such is the motivation behind the person who claims to be a loving devotee of one religious belief but who suddenly becomes a hating fanatic, as soon as he sees or hears a different opinion or concept of God. He loses all discrimination. In fact, such an individual has less understanding than a dog because a dog recognizes its master no matter what kind of suit the master is wearing.

The most hideous crimes have been committed in the name of religion and of love for the Lord. In their narrow-minded opinions and thoughts, certain sects think their beliefs are the only true ones, and they try to convince others of this. They kill thousands, and still they say, "Our religion is the only true one." How can people separate themselves so totally from their brothers and sisters that they can no longer recognize their own soul substance? How is it possible that we are driven so far away from each other that we don't feel our oneness anymore?

The cold attachment to a single concept that can lead to these tragedies is prevented when we walk upon the true path of love. This path of love, even though it may be childlike, is one of the most beautiful we can walk. It is the most natural path because it is that of knowing the unity of all things. This is the fullness of love that allows us to accept each other despite the labels we have given each other.

THE PATH OF LOVE BEGINS
IN LONELINESS AND PAIN

The starting point of this path of love is divine discontent, a vexation of the spirit. We feel an anguished hunger to unite with all creation. It is a craving feeling. You say, "It hurts me right in my heart. I love so much that it hurts."

What is it that we love so much? The world's religions have many names for it. But no matter what our religious backgrounds, we can feel the intense pain of our separation from the divine beloved, from God.

Because the divine beloved is all creation, it is also your fellow humans. We might not be capable of visualizing God in his totality, but we can see him in the eyes of our brothers and sisters. You have a hunger now, for you are separated from them, and you are separated from God. Soon after becoming aware of this yearning, you will begin to feel a great devotion. That devotion will help you to discipline yourself to the practices that will prepare you for the consummation of this love, divine union.

The preparations are not so simple as they sound. First, we must cleanse ourselves of our hates, our resentments, our fears, our anxieties, our jealousies, and our envies. This sanctification is the first step to the fulfillment of divine love arising out of divine discontent. Its purpose is to make one free to disassociate the inner self from those tangible things that stand contrary to God. It is a purity within and without, a self-cleansing process to become worthy of your natural environment, worthy to be part of this universal being, worthy of existing, worthy of understanding this existence.

We all know the most common ways to gain this purity; their laws are in the scriptures of all religions. Sadly enough, we don't follow them. They have become mere phrases that we use if we can get some profit out of them. On the path of love or any other path, the laws of spirituality should be followed. A person who lives righteously does not need human laws. Human laws have brought more suffering and injustice than help. If you live righteously, nobody has to tell you, "Thou shalt not steal" or "Thou shalt not kill."

Other steps on the path are cleanliness in thought and outer being, austerity, fasting, and prayer. By prayer, I do not mean asking; I mean affirming, acknowledging our own beings and our purposes of being. Through silent self-surrender to that inner being in meditation, we go within to find ourselves. By entering the within, we leave behind all worldly thoughts. The withdrawal of the senses and sense objects will make you calm, dispassionate, and single-hearted in purpose. Through concentration and meditation, it will bring the scattered energies and aims of life to a single focus on God, on the universe, and on yourself, when you reach the realization that you are god. Meditate upon that soul self, that universal self, that divine self.

There are some helpful means of attaining purification. One is the constant remembrance and repetition of the benevolent aspects of the universal being. The mantra, om, summons all the benevolent aspects. When we chant om, it is as though we are saying, "Thank you, Lord, for the flowers. Thank you for the birds and the oceans. Thank you for myself, that I am here." Repeat to yourself all the benevolent aspects: love, truth, mercy, aspiration. Never be satisfied; always remember more aspects each time.

You are actually training (or untraining) your subconscious

mind to start to break away the concrete that society has poured within you and now lies on your stomach as if you had swallowed all the boulders in the world. Transmute these solid masses into subtle forces. Break them down with the power of love, the highest vibration possible. Remember that the higher the vibration, the more subtle the mass. Nothing can withstand this high vibration, no matter how concrete it is; it will break down in the smallest particles possible. Release yourself from that block of concrete. Also, you can derive advantage from spiritual communion, interfusing and merging, with spiritually grown friends. They will emanate their divine love, and you will feel bliss, joy, peace when you are with these people.

When we meet our friends, we often say, "How are you?" Normally, before the friend can actually answer, we have turned our attentions away. We use so many words, but few have meaning or feeling. Have you ever waited for the reply? Have you ever thought how you might be capable of making them feel better if they are distressed? Do you ever realize how intolerant you are of others, when you throw out these words "How are you" without any interest in how they really are? Or is it that you are hungry for love yourself? You hope they will respond to your question by saying, "How are you?" Then you can show off all your problems because, of course, you expect them to listen to you. You have no time to listen to your friends, but you will expect them to stand there and listen to your whole tirade of pains and aches.

At first, we focus upon a devotional image, our image of God. Soon, we must look beyond. In its beginning stages, the path of love requires the vision of a beloved, an object of our loving. Because the relationship between the lover and the beloved has to be maintained at first on this plane of trial and error, there can hardly be devotion without the presence of a personal image of God. The aspirant to this path needs an object of love in space and time within the perception of his senses. He is too undeveloped to be able to direct his loving aim at a goal that remains unseen, unknown, impersonal, abstract, and transcendental. The adorational worship of God begins with the senses. The average beginner on this path needs a determined, limited form of God to soothe that initial vexation of spirit with a sense of truth.

To make an effort to comprehend the totality of the universe at the very beginning of the path can be self-defeating. At this stage, such a focus is just a meaningless abstraction. Rarely would it stimulate the flow of love energy needed to attain the goal. At this stage, we are still like children who need a picture in order to concentrate on a particular idea. Therefore, we create the image of a personal God. Those of us who no longer rely upon this image should not be too critical of those who still do. Although there is no man sitting in the clouds wearing a white robe, holding a big, fat book under his arm, and pointing his finger at you, many people need the guidance provided by this symbol. We should help them as best as we can to see the truth in the whole universe. In the beginning or preparatory stage, we often make use of images and symbols in order to develop. That explains the proper use of devotions to angels, saints, masters, and various representations of God. When you concentrate on that image from time to time, you feel the love. It is a remembrance.

Meditating on some of the aspects of God will bring us to the realization of the creative source. For example, a Buddhist devotional chant, "Om Mani Padme Hum," means "Hail, jewel in the lotus." The soul is like a jewel, like a diamond with a thousand facets. When we lift up a petal of the lotus blossom, a ray of the universal light enters and is reflected from one of these facets. That facet is love. The ray bounces back with tremendous energy into the universe. Soon, we will open another petal, and another aspect of God will become visible. Another ray of universal light falls upon the unveiled facet of the diamond, and it is reflected, is known. The chant teaches that we must wipe all the spider webs, all the dust, from our soul. We must remove all the veils that have been hiding the jewel and reveal it so that the universal God-light may be reflected in our beings.

Let your soul become the mirror of your being, reflecting all over the whole universe, touching us all, uplifting all those who walk in the dark, removing all the shadows of doubt. Let us disintegrate these shadows with the light of the rays from the jewel in the lotus. "Om Mani Padme Hum." This action is part of the path of integration.

Uniting all the aspects of God helps us to evolve from the need for a personal beloved to a striving for the impersonal, from symbols of God to the formless, absolute reality. The final fulfillment, of course, is the unity of lover, love, and beloved, in the supreme universal attainment. Then, the identity of God and the devotee is gained forever. We don't need to ask for an identification from God anymore. We will know the truth, for we will have experienced it in our own beings.

The basic elements leading to the attainment of divine love are renunciation, fearlessness, and selflessness. Renunciation means giving up the striving for material possessions and letting such possessions come as a fruit of your work. Love God, not for any reward, but for the sake of love and adoration. As God is omnipresent, so we must extend our love and adoration to everything and everyone in order to express the divine love.

Slowly, we will become intoxicated by this divine love. We will be able to perceive the beloved everywhere, in all creatures, in all the forms in nature. There will be no more intensely sensual visions and ecstasies. Our inner selves will glow from celestial love. Divine love will then become an experience that is ineffable.

As devotees of this path of love and integration, we will discard all reason and intellect, all cold logic and philosophy about God. We will know that our experiences are truths and that our realizations are not to be found in any theories or ideas. We will have complete faith based on our tremendous love and hunger to be one with universal being.

seven

LIVING THE
PATH OF ACTION

In my own life, I have learned that the path of love must be found and lived before any other. When its lessons have been understood, we are free to begin the path of action. Like the flower that disappears with the advent of the fruit, faith is lost in its fruition. Once we have expressed it and lived the truth that is its source, there is no need for faith. The result of actualizing faith is that we become completely conscious of our oneness with the whole cosmos. At all times, we know we are of the one. But our consciousnesses have not yet reached the level where we will attain understanding. This is why we speak of the pathways. Although we are never seperate from the whole, our awareness of this state is limited. We are somewhere on the path to understanding the totality of God. Some of us are sitting by the side of that path, waiting for other travelers to come and take us by the hand and lead us on. Others are on the way to pick up travelers.

Let us take this traveler by the hand and point out all the paths available rather than taking him or her on our path. Say, "See, friend, this is a path, that is another path, and there is yet another path. Make up your mind. I am tired of walking, but I have faith in my destination, so I will keep walking until I reach it. I cannot carry you on my shoulder. I have a hard enough time staying in my own shoes. Don't expect me to take you piggyback. Here is the road sign. Sit there in silence and find out what is in your own mind. Which path do you want to walk?" Know that on the horizon is the final result: your fruition, not just knowing that you are one with God, but experiencing that oneness, achieving the complete consciousness of it.

That is the path of action. It is the path based on right living. So many people imagine that they can say, "I have always lived right." Do they know what they are saying? Right living, right actions mean nonattachment. This path is not for people who intellectualize everything, nor for those who are solely emotional, nor for those who become sentimentally involved with spiritual realization.

Why don't people on the path of action become emotionally or sentimentally involved? It is because that is the path where we speak of a nonpersonalized focus, an impersonal God. We identify God, not with a person, but with a whole universe. We identify with all that exists, realizing that to be God is never perceiving anything as separate from ourselves.

The path of action lacks the predominant characteristic of the path of love, which has as its source the vexation of the spirit. On the path of action, you need no longer hunger to achieve union because you are never separated from God. You are always there. You just have to look into the eyes of another human being to see him. Through action, we know, rather than crave, the unity within all things.

You have only to shake hands with a fellow being to feel God. Pat or stroke your dog, and you pat and stroke God. Speak to the animals, and you speak to God. Inhale the fragrance of a flower, and you inhale the fragrance of God. See the drifting clouds, and you see God. All that exists is God omnipresent and omnipotent. God is not a specific image, not a personified entity.

It is not possible to know God in everything by analysis. You just have to know it, feel it, experience it. This path is meant for those people whose only aim in life is universal realization through active and practical application of their awareness of universal being.

This is an important concept. So many people who are seeking individual realization forget completely that it is impossible to realize an identity unless you have realized self first. The self, or God-self, is the substance of which you are created. When you know your substance, and when you know its qualities and aspects, then you can understand the particular forms it takes. If you start searching within yourself to discover your nature before knowing what your essence is, what will you find? Flesh and bones and a gray blob called the brain. That is all you will be able to perceive until you realize that your substance derives from the creative substance, that your essence is your God.

The qualities that you possess are individualized essential substance. Therefore, in order to become aware of your potentials, characteristics, and identity within this existence, you first have to find within yourself that which is eternal. On the path of action, this can be done only by the active, practical utilization of all God's aspects and qualities that you have discovered within yourself. This is an active, not a passive, way. On this path, we express our strivings in a different manner than we do on the path of love, with its passive, childlike faith. This faith is beautiful, but those who are on the path of action can no longer be content with faith. They cannot accept the idea that God is a person and that God will do everything for them if they just love him.

SELFLESS ACTION AND SERVICE

The New Testament says, "You are in this world, but not of this world." Those who are on this path know that they are in this world but also that they are not of this world. But that does not say it all; there is something lacking. There is more to it.

People who know this cannot sit and wait. They realize that they must act through service.

Traditional wisdom says that as long as you are in this world, you will have to serve this world by right actions, without evaluating the level on which fellow beings stand. The predominant characteristic of the path of action is a volitional spirit of selflessness or the spirit of will power. We cannot serve on the path of action if we are selfish.

What is my greatest selfishness? It is to recognize that through my selfishness, I reach selflessness. That sounds like a paradox, an enigma. My selfishness is in wanting to reach the end of that path as soon as possible, and I know that I can only attain it if I am completely selfless. The only true selfishness is striving to reach the goal. Therefore, I have labeled myself a selfish altruist. My selfishness is that I want to reach that goal, the horizon, God. I can only do it by being altruistic, by serving my fellow human beings, by showing them the paths. Some may sit and rest till they find which path they wish to follow. But I must keep active, guiding through service, through prayer, through healing, and through dedication, not to other people but to God, thereby including my fellow humans.

We must act on our knowledge of universal being and recognize all aspects of the cosmos without fear and without judgment. What would happen if two hours from now a flying saucer landed on a highway? How fast our tanks and missiles would be there to destroy it—out of pure fear! Pure fear is generated by ignorance, by not being active enough to know God and all his creatures. How can we be fearful of something that is created of divine substance? What can it take away from us? The most valuable of your possessions are your soul and your mind. They are imperishable. They can neither be taken away from you nor destroyed by any creature or form. Even God cannot take these from you. God cannot detract from you because you are a part of the substance of universal being. There is no such thing as destruction of a soul because that would be the universe destroying itself. This is why we live eternally.

Why do we have such a great fear of ending this existence? Because we fear that this existence is all there is. Do we not agree that soul is a part of universal being? Because God is eternal, soul is eternal. Do we not acknowledge that our bodies and minds are part of the universe? Anything that has ever been part of the universe is always part of it. So long as the universe exists, all its parts exist, making up its wholeness. Then why do we try to hold onto what is only a passing phase of this eternity? Why not fulfill the unique potential of mortal experience? In that phase, we have the opportunity to realize our creative powers and thus achieve the greatest fruition through actions of a volitional spirit.

We have to become selfless or have complete detachment of temper, which means that we cannot become emotionally involved. We become nonattached observers—sensitive to what is happening, but still observers.

How many people stop to smile at each other on a Sunday morning and say, "Good morning. Nice to see you in church," while in their thoughts they are totally occupied with disliking or envying their neighbors. We must stop indulging such behavior. Is organized religion merely for the purpose of building places in which to worship? We have come to act as if love and worship can exist only at specific times in specific places. This is not an attitude found on the path of action. That path teaches people to live with each other in an abiding relationship and to act accordingly.

The whole universe is our place of worship. How should we worship here? By action, by right living, and by right thinking, not by passing judgment, not by jealousy, and not by envy. This path teaches us always to remember our aim. For those who walk the path of action, there is only one horizon; nothing obscures that horizon, even though there are many obstacles along the way. They can look through and beyond the obstacles because they have only one aim: knowledge of and union with God. They never lose sight of that goal, no matter what weights they must carry on their backs. They are on this path to overcome through actions and through understanding. It is the path of inner development and inner improvement. That means, not putting a layer of new paint over old paint, but washing the old paint off and putting on a substantial new coat.

Those on the path of action are constantly changing inwardly; they are constantly working to improve their inner selves. They find satisfaction through inner development. It strengthens them and protects them in the outer world. It keeps them from becoming entangled in the illusory search for material goals. Whatever they find by improvement and development within themselves, they must bring forth in outward action.

The teaching of the ways of this path is directed toward our wills. Only by altering our inner attitudes through will power can we expand our awareness of spirit. It is easy to see the lack of significance of the external world when there is no involvement of the spirit. Without the involvement of the spirit, you are living an empty life, for you are not expressing your real self. The external world has no meaning unless we apply the lessons of the inner world in our actions. The inner world is the substance; from it, we can draw all the qualities, all the answers. And to find these aspects, we go into the silence. The most important work can be done in the silence following creative meditation.

What should you do when you find what you seek in the silence? Be quiet and observe. Do not analyze what is happening while you are in the silence. Just let it happen. Experience it through sight, sound, and feeling. When you return from this silence, grasp all the aspects with your conscious mind, and put them to work. The manifestation that took place within the silence should be utilized and applied through right action.

OUR ONE AIM MUST BE
INNER ATTAINMENT

Without guidance from the path of action, we can become involved and absorbed in what is nearest and most tangible, the external world. Too often, we find that our aims are directed toward the material world. We begin to believe that the more we can gain materially, the better we will be. We turn into pack rats. However, we soon learn that we cannot take our material gains with us when we move to the next level of consciousness. Consequently, all the striving for the achievement of material things in this life is senseless, particularly if material things are made the sole aim of life.

The truest aim is subtle and harder to attain, but it will make you happy and fill your heart with bliss. Every step you take brings joy, for you can sense that you are moving closer to your heart's desire, the creative source. That is the only significant aim: complete integration with the source, not only feeling one with it but also living and acting it. This path teaches you that although you may seem to be the one who is acting, you are really only the channel through which the power and energy of the creative source are passing. Those who practice this path will very soon understand that instead of molding their lives according to their wills, it is better to learn how to mold themselves to life. We have wasted so much energy trying to force life to be what we want it to be. We should allow life to transform us so that we become a reflection of life and thus the reflection of God.

Travelers following the path of action will not necessarily avoid pain, discomfort, unpleasantness, or suffering. They may not need to go out and purposely create it, either. In this world, we rarely need to do that. What we do not create ourselves, our brothers and sisters will create for us. What we must do is learn by it. We must accept these difficulties as challenges for action, and understand them, not just walk around them as though they did not exist. Overcome them by right action, by changing your inner attitudes toward these obstacles. Then you are creating higher vibrations. Every time you overcome an obstacle, it brings you closer to your goal because you have reached a higher level of consciousness and you will be that much closer to reaching your aim.

It might sound strange, but if these obstacles were not a part of life, the followers of this path would have to create such challenges so that they could develop strength by overcoming them. The challenges are required for the inner work and inner development that is necessary to reach the goal of inner attainment.

POSITIVE AND NEGATIVE KARMA

One characteristic of the path of action is that its travelers recognize the activity of fate or karma in their lives much more than anyone on another path. The universal law of cause and effect is one that is learned best on the path of action. Although fate or karma has a negative connotation, those on this path know that it is also the means by which progress can be made. We act, and the effect of this action comes back to us. We know more about the universe than we did before we acted. The results of our actions are our greatest teachers. But they shouldn't become stumbling blocks or hindrances on our way to attainment. We will have to understand that these things are lessons. You should never stop and say, "This is just my fate; it is just my karma." All your so-called natural talents, all your capacities, all your achievements are due to karma, to previous experiences, habits, and attitudes. You could not do what you do today without karma. It is the law of cause and effect.

Every tree that produces apples will have some of its apples eaten by worms. You might call them its negative karma. Yet, the tree will have many, many fruits that are pure and that carry within them the seeds for new trees. *Good luck* and *bad fortune* are words that show how ignorant we are about the law of cause and effect. Being lucky is not something happening to you in a random, blind way. You have caused the so-called luck. It is the fruit, the result of your actions; it is the effect of the cause.

Karma has two aspects: positive and negative. You do not

learn anything from the positive aspects. They are not the lessons; they are the fruits. The negative ones, the stumbling blocks, the obstacles on your path, are the lessons. The only way you can ever change things that disturb you is by acting, by doing something, by transmuting them. One of the reasons for taking physical, individual forms in the first place is that we each have the freedom to learn from our mistakes. Because the path of action teaches detachment of temper, I cannot just become angry at what is happening; I must expand my vision until I understand and am at peace with that aspect of my life.

On the path of action, we must gain the courage to expand beyond what we are. Let me give you an example. When I was fifteen years old, I became an apprentice window dresser. After working three months for the company, I became second window dresser. Then I worked for six years, interrupted by some years in prison camp, but, in total, six years. At this point, my boss called me in. I had just had my second raise that year. He said, "Jack, you had better look around for another job." I exclaimed, "What?! I have been getting two raises per year, so I must be valuable to the company." He continued, "That is just it. You are valuable to us. We took you as a fifteen-year-old boy, taught you, and made it so good for you that you do not want to leave us. But do you want to retire as a chief window dresser?" I was, as a matter of fact, ready to be promoted to chief window dresser. He said, "You're so secure, so happy with all these fringe benefits that you do not dare look in any other direction anymore. Now, if you start looking into another company that pays less, you might be chief window dresser for a year and then made manager of the store. After a year as manager of the store, you might move to another store and be made general manager of a whole chain of stores." My boss taught me an important lesson, one that I have tried to live by ever since. You have to have the courage to drop what is beautiful in the life you are living now in order to go on to a new challenge of life, a new action, a new service. You must dare to live courageously.

Once, when Saint Francis was on the battlefield, God spoke to him, saying, "Francis, drop your weapons and go home to rebuild my churches." So Saint Francis started to build churches. He began by collecting big rocks by the cartload. Finally, he and his helpers had enough. With his bare hands, he started to build a cathedral. After he completed the cathedral, he finally understood the meaning of God's words. God did not want more buildings; God wanted him to repair the real churches, those in people's hearts.

I, too, misunderstood. For years, I worked on the physical body of man with my hands, wasting forty-five minutes on each person. I did it for them instead of teaching them to do it for themselves. Finally, I dropped my physical therapy practice and started lecturing, teaching, and demonstrating full time.

During the first three months that I was working to set up my classes, there was not a penny of income. My wife said, "What are you doing? You had such a beautiful practice." This was true. But I knew that if I wanted to live my life rightly, I had to become what I had to become, no matter what sacrifice it would cost. The greatest reward is in knowing that you are doing the right thing, that which is right for you.

When on a journey to higher attainment, we cannot stop along the way and take forever to decide which path to follow. We have to make up our minds *now*. Although it may be that the paths we have just completed were very rugged, we should be glad that we completed them. We know that because of the experiences we had on former paths, we are better equipped for the next path, no matter what challenges it brings. This is why I say that I am never satisfied with my accomplishments, but always content. I find bliss and joy in the result of what I have done, no matter how difficult it was; but I am not satisfied, for satisfaction makes me lazy. I still have inner dissatisfaction because there is still more to be done, still more to be learned. My dissatisfaction will thrust me toward my horizon, reminding me that I have not reached it yet.

Influencing our karmas is not an external process; it is an inner process that changes our views of life. This change of inner attitude will be expressed in our external lives. Then we become examples for others, who may, through the change they see, eventually change themselves. Never try to change the world. Give up trying to change others. Change yourself. If you do not like a person, that is your problem. You cannot change him; you can only change your inner attitude. Change yourself, and the world changes by itself. Recognize that you cannot take all the problems of the world on your shoulders. Then you will have the energy actually to do something rather than just worry about your inability to change the world. You must finally shoulder your real responsibility, which is to face your own problems and work them out.

We seem to be most intolerant toward those closest to us. In marriage, we try to change our partners until it hurts them. They are trying to do the same thing to us. That is foolish. Instead, we should each try to change ourselves. Then we would not only waste less energy but would have much better understanding, much more peace, much more love, and much more harmony. At some time or other, we have all had someone say to us, "How can you say things like that to me? I thought you loved me." As if that had anything to do with it! Have you ever noticed that you are saying it *because* you love? If you did not love the person, you would ignore him or her. There is a saying, "The ones you love, you hurt the most." You should not hesitate to use your scalpel on them, but do not try to change them. Help them to become aware of their failings, not through criticism, but through caring evaluation.

I have always believed that those who tell me my failures are really my friends. My enemies are those who tell my failures to my friends. To these enemies, I send the most love, for they need my love. Have you ever realized that you always give love to the wrong people? You always love those to whom you are attracted. But they do not need it. Your love is already with them. Your enemies really need your love to be given them because they lack it entirely.

CREATIVE IMPROVISATION

We each play a role in life. If we put our whole selves into them, we become those roles. We become those characters; we live them. My role in life is to know that I am an actor on a divine stage. I want to live it in every movement and fiber of my being. I want to be the character that is written for me, for I am a part of a divine plan. But even though my script says "stage left," there is no one preventing me from standing "stage right." I can improvise. This is what I mean when I say that we are instruments that can self-create by our power to adapt ourselves to every situation in life. Only those who have no recognition of that power will be incapable of creative improvisation. Such people are not actors; they are only spectators. Even though they may become sentimentally involved, they are not living in the way that those who are aware that they are the actualization of the divine plan are living. It is the most beautiful thing to be an actor on the stage of the cosmos. Then the living of life teaches us to mold ourselves. It is our choice to mold ourselves toward life, to not become stagnated by circumstances. We can look at circumstances and improvise. That is how to become creative and to awaken.

That is what life is all about, to be on the stage, not to be just a spectator in the audience. We must realize how much we are influenced by the other aspects of the play. In the prenatal stage of life, we are surrounded by people, things, and events that emanate their thoughts and vibrations. Knowingly and unknowingly, they affect our beings. In the later stages of life, we are subjected to environment, education, society, partners, tastes, customs, and tradition. We must maintain our awareness of these influences and also our awareness of our own roles. Then we will understand that it is impossible to be a spectator. By this perception, we can see how we can change the attitudes we have acquired and thus affect the roles others play. The only thing we can change is ourselves. When we change our attitudes toward others, they, in turn, will change automatically, and we will look at them differently.

Some people say, "I hate and despise my life. But I do not dare to change it because I do not know what the new life will be." Because of this fear, many people have not really lived. We do not need to worry. When a child fails a course, we give him a chance to do it over and over again until he finally learns. Do you think that a universal creative power could be so limited that it would provide us with only one chance to learn? That could not be so. You do not have to believe in reincarnation, for within one lifetime, there are as many opportunities for growth as we have the courage to face. We must not fear change; we must welcome it as the chance to progress to clearer perception and a potentially fuller state of being. It seems to me that we do not require the memory of former lives to know that there must be more than just one short episode of life. Even though you may be seventy-five or eighty-five years old, this period that you have lived is only a fraction of a second in the life of the universe. Life and death are only a falling asleep and an awakening. Only to you, in your present identity, does one lifetime seem like a long period. When you put your mind and altered attitudes into action, time no longer exists for you. Clocks are not important anymore. If you are part of the wholeness that is the universe, how can you be destroyed? When you are awake to this unity, there is no fear of failure or of death. These are known for what they are: steps on the journey to reunion.

Those who follow the path of nonattachment apply that nonattachment to everything that affects them externally. By doing this, they find peace of mind and soul. They are completely free from the dictates of the outside world. Like actors, they play their roles in life with a conscious emphasis on the characterization of righteous action.

To be in this world yet not of this world means that everyone following the path of action should perform their duties on *all* levels of life, physical, mental, and spiritual. It is true that most human beings are involved solely in acting out their physical duties and, to a certain degree, their mental ones. But without any involvement of spirit or any real understanding of what spirit is, both are merely automated reactions.

We speak of proper actions, but what do we mean? If we are aware of the meaning, are we acting accordingly? Let us determine what proper action is. We realize that we have to see the individual as a whole. There are two ways of understanding this. It sounds like "hole" when I say it, but I mean "whole." Too often, a person becomes an empty hole in the universe instead of a whole. Instead we should become *w-h-o-l-e* and deal with everyone as whole beings. It should be very clear that right action involves our whole beings, their mental, spiritual, and physical manifestations. We should never be satisfied with expressing only one or two of these aspects. Even if we have reached quite a high level of understanding or awareness and act on our spiritual and mental levels, that is not enough. You can know something spiritually and mentally, but if you do not act it and express it in your physical life, you are lopsided. You have to act it out in your own life both externally and internally.

We will have to go through much effort in order to be an example of the spiritual life by activating the mind to express it in the physical life. We need a conscious physical expression to bring spirituality into proper action. This is true whenever we act. In order to be in harmony or to reach an equilibrium, we need the involvement of all three aspects. A scale without a fulcrum can weigh nothing.

On this path, we are required to materialize the visions of meditation in practical actions. These visions are messages from a higher level of consciousness. Someone else's consciousness? No, your consciousness, too. There is only one consciousness that reveals itself in individuals: the universal consciousness. You think of yourself as being a drop of water, but recognize that you are also the whole ocean. Change the drop of water, and you thereby change not only the drop of water but the whole ocean. By changing yourself, you are changing the level of consciousness in the complete universe.

Don't always speak of your own consciousness, for just the slightest movement of your finger sends this whole universe into a different motion. Every thought, every action that you express pertains not just to you but to all beings and to all levels of consciousness in the total universe. Let these thoughts and deeds be of positive action. You will create a higher level of consciousness not only in yourself but in everything that has its life and being in the whole universe. You should never hold back these divine expressions of being because you think you lack the creativity to express them. These visions are not meant to stay in storage in our subconscious minds. Their high energy can be released to pervade and transform this world only when they are actively expressed in our lives.

At one time, divine visions were revealed only to mystics and saints. That time is over. We should all be saints and mystics. After all, what is a saint or a mystic? One who lives spiritually in every thought and action. Put your energy, your mind, and finally your heart into every action. Do all things with love, and you will get joy out of all that you do. Joy is the seed that contains bliss. Blessed are those who are capable of bringing their heart into every action. They are true mystics. Open your eyes. Look into the eyes of your fellow human beings. In particular, look into the eyes of youth. If you cannot discover the mystic vision in their eyes, you must be blind.

Let our eyes be turned inward to the God-self to perceive the power needed to bring this new mysticism into being. If we indeed want a new world, we had better start creating it right now. Let us recognize these new mystics, not the ones walking among us in robes and white collars. The true mystics activate the spark of love within you by their beings and their actions. That spark is not a personal feeling of love but the complete universal emotion. Through that emotion we will gain the ability and the power to make the material world a spiritual world. We must practice what comes to us in meditation and what we learn from any source of communication with God. We should have communication with God twenty-four hours a day. Communication with God means living with nature as a cocreator, with every particle of your being every moment of your life. Every action should be communication with God. "Know ye not that ye are Gods?" Do not separate yourself from the God-self. Do not be proud about it. Recognize it, be grateful. Have understanding for others as they, too, struggle for realization.

Have no secrets. Share what you are receiving within yourself. I know the hardest part of this sharing is that most of the time the experiences are ineffable. You cannot find the words to express them. That is not important. Express them in action. Share them with others so that they can grow with you. That is the important thing. Don't judge anyone to be ready for your insights or not. Give them what you can give, without regard to their levels of being. We must share this glory with others in order to make them more and more aware so that they will start searching within themselves for truth. When they find this truth, they, too, will express it in the world and will not keep it a secret, hidden in their inner selves. When I say that we should share these visions, I do not mean that we should tell people everything we see or hear during our meditations. We do not need more rhetoric or prideful displays; we need more spiritual action. We will exemplify to others how we are changing and growing by our actions, and we have more compassion for them in this way.

THE PATH OF ACTION IS A PATH OF NONATTACHMENT

I have talked about nonattachment, but I have not given any directions for how to achieve it. I have a series of very simple-sounding rules for the attainment of nonattachment. However, experience has taught me that our physical and materialistic outlooks make it a little difficult to follow them. It might be a good idea to study them extensively before bringing them into practice. And to be effective, this study should be done without excitement or desire for gain.

1. Never become depressed by the prospect of loss or failure. That is one of the hardest things to learn. After putting everything into what is seemingly a loss or failure, you may not see that this failure is actually your profit. It creates a new challenge to do better next time. Remember, your successes can be put aside. They are already fruit. Your so-called failures reactivate your inner being to do better, to be loyal to your greatest potentials, thereby sowing seeds for the next harvest.

2. Learn to express yourself. You are not creative enough? Paint, play music, write, sing, dance, engage in dialogue. You think you have no background for it? What kind of background do you want? Do you want to have all kinds of diplomas hanging on the wall to show what you have earned? Why don't you paint? Are you afraid that neighbors might not like your painting? Then you are attached to their opinions. Suppose someone says, "Oh! That looks terrible. You call that a painting?" Does that matter to you? It may look terrible to them, but if you have put your soul on that canvas, if you have expressed your soul in paint, it does not matter how it looks. What matters is how it feels to you because you are expressed in those colors and forms. You have actualized something of yourself on that piece of canvas with paint. Suppose that you write words that came not by conscious thinking but were unknowingly within yourself. No one understands them? It sounds like abracadabra? That does not matter. You have put some of your soul down on the paper. By doing that, you have made yourself immortal. Dare to live, to express yourself in the manner that is best for you. Do not hold back because of others' beliefs, philosophies, or rigid instructions.

3. Universalize your aims and purposes. In other words, you should not work only for yourself; you should have universal

aims. Think about the whole universe and about what you are. You *are* the universe. You are a part of it. Therefore, every action you create should be toward that whole universe, not toward you as a little part of it. Recognize yourself to be the whole universe. Know that through individuality, what you are creating within yourself is for the entire universe.

4. Always be aware that it is not you who do the work, that it is the creative source within you. You are, or should be, a free channel so that this source within you is being expressed, rather than your separate personal identity. You should always remember that this personal identity is not the source of actions. You are always working with spirit. It is only through the creative substance, the spirit that flows through you, that you can work at all. You are an instrument that is formed of the three aspects of life.

These rules will help to diminish the pains that accompany the consequences of our fates. Following these rules will cause cessation of fate or karma. As nonattached travelers, realizing the real "I" and the real "thou," we will know our true natures to be God and will cease to bind ourselves with attachments. A false sense of "I" and "mine" characterizes the personality of an egocentric. After the limitations of the "I" and "mine" attitude have been transcended, we will expand and embrace the impersonal universal being as a service to humankind. We should surrender the fruits of our works to the universe. Everyone should share in the fruits of your work.

Above all, you must do this with sincerity. You must dedicate every action of your life to the attainment of the universal aim. Open your heart to hear the voice of the God-self within. Express its wisdom through your thoughts and deeds, not for self-gratification, but to aid all others on the path. Then you will be on the path of action.

Note

Jack Schwarz plans to establish in Gold Hill, Oregon, a spiritual, psycho-physical therapeutic complex where human beings can develop to the extent of optimal, spiritual, psychological, and physical health—wholeness. Such a place will be like a "medicine wheel" with many spokes to provide a multi-dimensional, all-inclusive, diagnostic, therapeutic training center existing and working in a broad framework of holistic methods, alternative methods of healing, preventive methods, and maintenance of optimal health adapted from many other cultural traditions as well as our own already available sources.

For further information, please contact:

Aletheia Psycho-Physical Foundation
515 N.E. 8th Street
Grans Pass, Oregon 97526

DUTTON PAPERBACKS OF RELATED INTEREST

Philosophy and Religion:

THE MIND OF LIGHT, Sri Aurobindo
BEYOND THE GODS, John Blofeld
I-CHING: THE BOOK OF CHANGE, John Blofeld
THE SECRET AND SUBLIME: TAOIST MYSTERIES AND MAGIC, John Blofeld
THE TANTRIC MYSTICISM OF TIBET: A PRACTICAL GUIDE, John Blofeld
AMONG THE DERVISHES, O. M. Burke
ANOTHER WAY OF LAUGHTER, Massud Farzan
THE TALE OF THE REED PIPE, Massud Farzan
TRANSCENDENTAL MEDITATION, Jack Forem
BEELZEBUB'S TALES TO HIS GRANDSON (ALL AND EVERYTHING, *First Series*), G. I. Gurdjieff
MEETINGS WITH REMAKABLE MEN (ALL AND EVERYTHING, *Second Series*), G. I. Gurdijieff
VIEWS FROM THE REAL WORLD, G. I. Gurdjieff
THE AWAKENING OF KUNDALINI, Gopi Krishna
RADHAKRISHNAN, Robert McDermott, editor
LIFE AT ITS BEST, Meher Baba
THE BHAGAVAD GITA, Geoffrey Parrinder
ONLY ONE SKY, Bhagwan Shree Rajneesh
TEACHINGS OF RUMI, Jalaluddin Rumi
THE WALLED GARDEN OF TRUTH, Hakim Sanai
THE SECRET GARDEN, Mahmud Shabistari
THE DERMIS PROBE, Idries Shah
THE EXPLOITS OF THE INCOMPARABLE MULLA NASRUDIN, Idries Shah
THE MAGIC MONASTERY, Idries Shah
ORIENTAL MAGIC, Idries Shah
THE PLEASANTRIES OF MULLA NASRUDIN, Idries Shah
THE SUBTLETIES OF THE INIMITABLE MULLA NASRUDIN, Idries Shah
TALES OF THE DERVISHES, Idries Shah
THE WAY OF THE SUFI, Idries Shah
WISDOM OF THE IDIOTS, Idries Shah
THE ELEPHANT IN THE DARK, Idries Shah and others
THE SPIRIT OF THE EAST, Ikbal Ali Shah
MYSTICISM, Evelyn Underhill
THE KAMA SUTRA, Vatsyayana
SUFI STUDIES: EAST AND WEST, Rushbrook Williams